Praying the Prophets

Mining the Old Testament Prophets
For Daily Leadership Guidance

John P. Chandler

Illustrated by Jessica Luttrull

Foreword by Alan Hirsch and Mike Breen

Isaiah - Malachi

Published by *Uptick Imprint,* 4 Lee Court, Lake Monticello, Virginia, 22963, USA.

All Scripture quotations are taken from The New Oxford Annotated Bible containing the Old and New Testaments, edited by Bruce M. Metzger and Roland E. Murphy, New Revised Standard Version, Oxford University Press, New York, NY, 1991, 1994.

Design: Jessica Luttrull
USA ISBN-13: 978-0-9890816-4-1
Printed in the United States of America. First printing, 2013.

Library of Congress Cataloguing-in-Publication Data
Chander, John, 1961-

Praying the Prophets: Mining the Old Testament Prophets for Daily Leadership Guidance

ISBN-13: 978-0-9890816-4-1
1. Leadership; 2. Guidance; 3. Discipleship; 4. Old Testament

What others are saying about the "Praying ..." Series

"John's gift of helping leaders look at their role through the lenses of scripture is a gift that is beyond measure. This book is a sacred offering to those who have been called and entrusted to lead. Seasoned leaders and emerging leaders will be inspired to lead others in "the way" that will provide the most significant imprint a leader can leave – the imprint of Christ."

Jan Bazow
Founder and CEO, Fortis Group | Richmond, Virginia

"Some pontificate on leadership without actually getting their hands dirty leading. Some leverage leadership ideals to boost their ego rather than to lay down their life for God's Kingdom. It's rare to find someone who surrenders themselves to the tiresome work of leading with both humility and courage. Even rarer is when this person can also guide us along the same path. John Chandler is one of these rare leaders."

Winn Collier
Author, Holy Curiosity | Pastor, All Souls Charlottesville | Charlottesville, Virginia

"John Chandler is the kind of guy I from which I want to learn about Scripture. He knows and loves the Bible. He understands our world. He studies leadership (and leads well himself). And he cares about people. Working through the reflections, I've seen first-hand how John's combination of scholarship and experience makes "Praying" simple but not simplistic, scholarly but not pedantic, and inspirational but not sappy."

Travis Collins
Author, Tough Calls | Pastor, Bon Air Baptist Church | Richmond, Virginia

"John Chandler is a follower of Jesus who will captivate you as he takes you on a personal journey through God's word. He will challenge your thinking and call you to act on the same verses that led to the God stories we all love! As someone who has had the privilege of being before Kings, there is no experience greater than being in the presence of the King of Kings. John is a personal friend and a leader who demonstrates Christ-like love. I know he will inspire you as he has me, to live out God's word."

Jimmie Davidson
PEACE Pastor, Saddleback Church, California | Founding Pastor of Highlands Fellowship, Abingdon, Virginia

"There is no compromise for principle-based leadership and John's "Praying" books are extraordinarily inspiring. These books give each of us insight which can be applied not only to our roles as leaders, but also importantly, who we are as followers. John is truly one of our most prized thought leaders and I am left inspired following every interaction I have with him. These are books I will keep at my side and recommend to all who humbly strive to lead and follow as God would have us do."

Tiffany Franks
President of Averett University | Danville, Virginia

"Working with college students, I know the importance of quick and memorable coffee house communication. Jessica Luttrull has an artist's knack for communicating complex concepts in ways that are catchy, memorable, and even profound. Pair that with John Chandler's concise discoveries of biblical wisdom and you get an elegant, potent, and useful daily handbook for growing as a biblical leader."

Evan Hansen
Director of Eunoia | www.beautifulthinking.org | Charlottesville, Virginia

"John Chandler has shaped countless ministers through his tireless commitment leadership development. I am blessed to be one of them. As a leader of leaders, many of whom have no formal biblical training, I am grateful for this leadership development tool. John has made biblical wisdom accessible, impactful and memorable for Christians at all levels of leadership and all stages of spiritual maturity. Visual learners like me will love the drawings that anyone can replicate as they share these nuggets of wisdom with others."

Wendy McCaig
Author, From the Sanctuary to the Streets | Founder and Executive Director, Embrace Richmond | Richmond, Virginia

"I have been studying the Bible now for over six decades, and I am continually amazed at the fresh insights God provides me each time I open His book. In his "Praying" books, my good friend John Chandler also provides some fresh, practical insights into how to make your Bible study more productive and how to become a better leader in the process.

Focusing on the Old Testament, particularly the rich history of Israel and its kings and leaders, John reviews a chapter, highlights a truth and then makes a practical application.

Read this book because it's witty, insightful, and practical, but also read this book because it is written by a proven leader who knows what he is talking about, who has dealt with the enormous challenges of training young ministers to be more effective in advancing the kingdom in a culture that, morally, looks very similar to Israel during the reign of its kings and leaders over 3000 years ago.

John's leadership of Spence Network has transformed the lives of many young ministers and better prepared them to take on the challenges of leading the church in the 21st Century. I have seen the result of John's work first hand in the transformed lives of many young leaders he has invested in; his book may transform your life as well."

Bob Russell
Author, When God Builds a Church | Bob Russell Ministries |
Louisville, Kentucky

"The power of the Baptist movement in history is its belief that any person has access to the heart of God through Jesus Christ. When we humbly submit ourselves to the Bible and see ourselves reflected there, we can trust that the Holy Spirit will speak to us, and that we can hear, respond, and lead. This is one reason I am excited that my friend and fellow leader John Chandler has written these leadership devotionals. These reflections are both suitable for presidents, and for ordinary folk on church nominating committees. They will help anyone who wants to lead biblically and lead well. It is my hope that every Baptist in Virginia and around the world who has to make decisions will use John's book to turn their hearts to the God of the Bible who can give wisdom for daily leading. Trust me, you will be changed and you will be a better leader!"

John Upton
Executive Director, Baptist General Association of Virginia | President, Baptist World Alliance | Richmond and Falls Church, Virginia

"Great Bible exegesis is only truly great when it spans the millennia to inform and inspire our world today. John Chandler has that unique ability to interpret scripture with integrity and application. Moreover John's own walk with Jesus matches the words he brings to print. I thoroughly commend John's writings to anyone looking to strengthen their walk with Jesus.

Craig Vernall
National Leader. Baptist Churches of New Zealand | Tauranga, New Zealand

"John Chandler has provided a key ingredient in the formation of any effective congregational leader: regular, consistent, insightful and inspiring study of scripture. His insights are simple, yet profound. His approach is extremely user-friendly and accessible. His knowledge of congregational life is not naïve or divorced from reality. I am grateful for this powerful addition to our efforts to raise up leaders for God's people in the 21st century."

Bill Wilson
President, Center for Congregational Health | Winston-Salem, North Carolina

Dedication

To John Vincent Upton, fearless leader, boss extraordinaire, creative leader, and someone who embodies the Virginia Baptist calling to advance the Kingdom and lead from a global platform;

And to all of my Virginia Baptist fellow workers – all of you apostles, prophets, evangelists, pastors, and teachers who lead with humor, grace, vision, and a lot of fun;

Thank you for leading like progressive prophets, rooted in the Bible, bound in twenty-first century community, and full of joy. You all make me so proud to be a part of this tribe!

Table of Contents

Foreword to the "Praying" series

By Alan Hirsch and Mike Breen

Those who would reactivate the missional church must first awaken a missional form of discipleship. Clearly, it will take the whole people of God – apostles, prophets, evangelists, pastors, and teachers – to catalyze a movement of the Kingdom of God in the West. We are long past the day of believing that this movement can rest alone in the hands of superstar preachers and celebrity Christians. Every revolution is led by an uprising of peasants, not the edict of kings. And the revolution of Jesus' Kingdom breaking in on earth as it is in heaven is no different. It will take place when ordinary disciples lead the church in the world.

But where are all of these ordinary apostles, prophets, evangelists, shepherds, and teachers going to come from? From disciples who are becoming more acculturated to the ways of Jesus than tamed by pervasive cultural mores. And they are going to become acculturated to Jesus' forgotten ways by learning a rhythm of daily engagement with his presence.

The early church exploded from a minor sect to a world movement when it embraced an "all-hands-on-deck" missional form of living and leading – that is, when *every* follower of Jesus did the heavy lifting. Ordinary people had to act as apostles, prophets, evangelists, shepherds, and teachers. No one sat on their hands and waited for the twelve famous people who walked with Jesus to do all of the leading. And if we want to see the West today transformed from dying Christendom to a reawakened missional movement of the Kingdom of God, then it will take all of us being better leaders. The only way we become better leaders is by becoming better followers, better listeners. We are all going to have to embrace a spirituality that learns to listen to and follow the God of the Bible.

If you want to sit around at Sunday lunch and argue that if your preacher would only preach a little better, then all would be well, you are sadly mistaken. Sure, better preaching is helpful. But alone, your pastor is not enough, and preaching is clearly not enough. It will barely budge the church, let alone the neighborhood – or the world, for heaven's sake! It doesn't all depend on platform people. It depends on all of us being disciples, and on disciples being leaders.

This is why I am so excited about John Chandler's series of books that demonstrate a path for praying through the Bible. Even better, these are excellent, mature, articulate, and distinctly *adult* types of reflection. There is a scholarly depth and social breadth beneath the concise and understandable applications of Scripture. But though academically and theologically sound (and at times profound), what we come out with when we read these reflections is *clarity*. Things are clear enough that I can scribble them down on a napkin and show you something that might inform a decision you have to make that day. We learn to listen to the Bible with the full expectation that God will speak to us. And as God speaks to us and leads us, we become more capable of leading others as well.

The "*Praying*" books have credibility because they already have had impact on groups of young adult leaders that John leads called "*Uptick*." It is part of the training: they learn from John how to engage with the Bible and catch the rhythm of discipleship, learn to live dynamically engaging God's Kingdom in the world. This in turn has been part of reshaping his tribe, Virginia Baptists, into one of the most refreshing and innovative denominations I have experienced in the last few years. As James Davison Hunter has written, movements that "change the world" start through activating small, tight networks. Jesus himself said that the Kingdom of heaven is like a mustard seed. Amazing things happen when ordinary leaders live as listening disciples.

I know that John has shared this kind of teaching with some of the most powerful and influential leaders in the world. But what I really like is that this kind of "octane" is available to ordinary disciples. This is not just a book for pastors; this is a book for *you and me*. If you will begin to catch the rhythm of listening to the God of the Bible by following John's lead, you will become a better disciple and a better leader."

Alan Hirsch
Author | Activist | Dreamer
The Permanent Revolution, Untamed, The Forgotten Ways, The Shaping of Things to Come

Here's the thing: Without a proper rhythm of life, it is impossible to hear the voice of God and experience the leading of the Holy Spirit. Going "OUT" to the world or "IN" to your close relationships without the "UP" of daily listening to God lapses into empty activism or self-indulgence. Until we learn to abide and await direction from the Word of God in Scripture, we are, in Paul's words, little more than *"noisy gongs or clanging cymbals"* (1 Corinthians 13:1).

In saying this, I could not be more pleased that my friend John Chandler has written this *"Praying"* series through the Old Testament. Understand from the outset, this isn't an attempt to cover every chapter of the Old Testament. He is not trying to offer the final, definitive picture of what God says there. Far from it. He is instead inviting you to *join him* in his practice of listening to God, participating in the "UPward" relationship of abiding, resting, pausing, waiting, and listening – which usually precedes a word from God. **If you learn to do that in these selected chapters, you will learn to do so in many other chapters not covered here.**

Take the example of learning to ride a bicycle. Maybe you were taught to ride by a parent, sibling or friend who walked beside you as you started unsteadily. Walking alongside you slowly at first, then guiding until you gained momentum and confidence, they then let you go. The steering became easier as you learned to pedal more rapidly. And once you learned to ride a bike, you never forgot. This is what John is trying to do in these reflections. He is modeling the way, walking alongside of you, helping you gain speed – and he will let you go in order to explore on your own the rest of the Bible in all of its riches.

At least in my understanding, this is one of the most biblical ways of teaching. Jesus drew his disciples around him so they could learn by watching. Paul repeatedly said to his churches, "*Imitate me as I imitate Christ*" (1 Corinthians 11:1, Philippians 3:17, 2 Thessalonians 3:7, Hebrews 13:7, etc.). John himself has a track record of offering his life and leadership to other disciples so that they can learn to grow in the rhythms of Jesus. And in this book, he is offering a way of imitation to you. We never get to innovation by mere information; it takes imitation as well. And if you will learn to imitate John's practice of listening daily to the Bible and expecting God to guide you, you will grow as a disciple of Jesus.

Maybe we can use a quick example.

Many of us have probably had someone in our church community approach us with a measure of frustration and say, "Can you help me read this book? No matter how much I try, I can't seem to understand what I read in the Bible. It doesn't always make sense." What do most of us do? Well, we probably give them a book that was particularly helpful for us; maybe we ask some questions; but we probably also show them *how we engage with the scriptures!* That's what we are talking about here. There's information we give, but then we flesh it out with a real-life example. We realize that the purpose of imitation is that it will lead to innovation.

I am particularly excited for the visual material accompanying these reflections. Don't let the simple nature of the sketches fool you. Their power is found not only in how they capture the big idea of the reflection. The drawings are powerful because they enable you to understand and pass along that big idea to another person. Again, true discipleship is not merely listening "UP" to God or taking information "IN" to your own heart. Until we pass along the word of God out to others, we have not "closed the circuit." And these illustrations will help you lead "OUT" by giving you a concrete way of sharing what you have heard. *It makes it reproducible!*

In my own experience, having visual material (LifeShapes) is a way of helping people who learn by sight and by touch in a different way than conceptual learners. Art makes material available to a whole different group of people, and perhaps to a whole different sector of your heart. These sketches are catchy, memorable, and portable. They can be cross-cultural and cross-generational. The artist, Jessica Luttrull, has done us a favor. She has made her work repeatable. By offering art that we can sketch to others, she has created a vehicle for us to grow in being disciples and making disciples.

In short, I hope you will not only read the book, but learn to imitate the way that is modeled here: to listen expectantly, discern clearly, and lead biblically. John is an apostolic leader, and I am seeing evidences of "torches" he is lighting with young leaders ("Uptick") and other Virginia Baptists who are imitating him as he imitates Christ. They are growing and paying it forward by teaching others to be disciples of Jesus. We want to see these torches become "bonfires," missional centers not only in Virginia, but around the world. I pray that as this book helps you set your rhythm of life with Jesus, your life will become a torch that will become a part of this larger bonfire.

Mike Breen
Global Leader, 3D Ministries | Pawleys Island, South Carolina
Author, *Building a Discipling Culture, Covenant and Kingdom*

Preface: *How this book began*

I experienced the great blessing of growing up in a time and place where reading the Bible was intrinsically valued as the path to personal transformation. If you wanted to know and grow with the God of Jesus Christ, then the first and best way to do that was to study the Bible.

My grandfather would quietly mention that he read entirely through a different translation of the Bible every year. My blind grandmother would listen to recorded cassette tapes of scripture and often memorize entire chapters at a time. In my Sunday School at Friendly Avenue Baptist Church in Greensboro, North Carolina, we turned in weekly offering envelopes with checkmark answers to the personal question, "Bible Read Daily?" Once I became a teenage disciple of Jesus Christ, I learned to read at bed time my "Good News" version of the Bible, with its simple but interesting stick-figure illustrations.

Bible study which began as an adolescent conviction then developed into adult academic pursuit at the university and seminary, and later a vocational habit as a pastor and teacher. I have since experimented with creative ways to continue engaging with the Bible diligently, such as listening to spoken scripture while riding my motorcycle. Leviticus is never as interesting as when blared at eighty miles an hour!

Several years, ago, my friend Mike Breen challenged me about the discipline of "winning the first battle of the day" – that is, to engage in listening conversation with God through the Bible before turning to the inbox and my work for that day. I decided to do away with my first-thing-in-the morning habit of two newspapers and ESPN SportsCenter, and devote myself instead to serious, daily reflection on one chapter of Scripture every day. With strong coffee and my cat at my side, I began to consolidate lessons and sermons from a quarter-century's worth of previous teaching alongside of new study, and to record the key notes in the margins of a single preaching Bible. What I initially feared would be an hour or two I couldn't spare every day became the best practice I undertook, as I became a calmer, clearer, more effective leader. As my personal muscle for the practice developed, so did my ability to lead others to do likewise.

A relational network is a powerful thing, and through one such network, I met a very important leader, one whose daily decisions impact untold numbers of people. The short version of the story is that my wife, Mary, and I began to pray daily for him. And I began to email this leader two to four brief reflections from the Old Testament as I studied every day. I tried to hone in on leadership insights and how a chapter might give guidance for daily decisions such leaders face. Whenever God impressed something upon me through daily study, I captured it in a brief email, and sent it forward.

I found this idea of leadership guidance to be a fascinating lens through which to engage with the Bible. I also found that whatever guidance I sent to this leader was often useful to share with others. Often I would diagram on the back of a napkin a simple picture to capture the core daily insight. Over time, as I tried to lead, teach, and mentor, this became a habit. After a year's worth of doing so, Mary suggested that I compile these reflections into a book.

There are 929 chapters in the Old Testament and I focused selectively and not comprehensively on some of what God had to say about leadership within the 250 chapters between Isaiah and Malachi. The title, **Praying the Prophets,** is a nod to the reality that often the best leaders in these chapters are not kings and people in position and title, but outsiders, the unpopular, and ordinary people without post or public recognition - but leaders nonetheless. This work starts in the book of Isaiah, where the prophet unhesitatingly speaks truth to power. It ends in the book of Malachi, gateway to the promise of a Messiah, Jesus, who would once and for all demonstrate true leadership. Between Isaiah and Malachi are many demonstrations of what makes for good and bad leadership. What I share here only scratches the surface. I believe that anyone who will engage in disciplined listening to the prophetic material will find many more (and better) insights about leadership than are captured here!

While I want these specific devotions to guide leaders in daily decisions, I hope even more deeply that they model the way to form habits or "build the muscles" of disciples to listen every day to God through scripture. When leaders are habitually disciplined to engage with the Bible about their leadership, they will be amazed at the guidance that comes from God. It is *new every morning* (Lamentations 3:23). I am certainly finding this to be true, as the verse with which my grandfather charged me at ordination to ministry is unfolding in my life:

> *"The Lord God has given me the tongue of a teacher, that I*
> *may know how to sustain the weary with a word. Morning*
> *by morning he wakens – wakens my ear to listen as those*
> *who are taught." – Isaiah 50:4*

I pray this work will help to waken your ear as you lead.

John P. Chandler

Introduction: *Goals, Audience, Methods*

Goals

The premise for this book is a simple one: reading the Bible expectantly can change your life as a leader. If you will discipline yourself to come to Scripture every day with the conviction that God will offer concrete guidance for your life and leadership, you won't be disappointed. There will be "fresh bread" given to you as surely as God gave Israel manna in the desert. And, when you learn to capture these biblical insights in simple pictures and pass them "on the back of a napkin" to other leaders, you will unlock great power for yourself and for many.

My goal is to model the way for you to do this so that you can build the muscle to make it the time signature in your rhythm of life.

Mike Breen teaches brilliantly of the imagery of the work of finding wisdom. Citing Job 28, he says that our job is to "dig" or "excavate" the precious gold of wisdom under the surface. Sometimes wisdom simply comes to us through an <u>eruption</u> of the Holy Spirit, like lava from beneath the earth's surface spouting from a volcano. Other times, we gain wisdom the hard way – through <u>erosion</u>, where suffering strips away the topsoil of our life, revealing precious but hard-won metals underneath. But beyond eruption and erosion is a third way: the way of <u>excavation</u>. Here, we dig a shaft beneath the surface soil until we find the gold underneath.

Here's a picture:

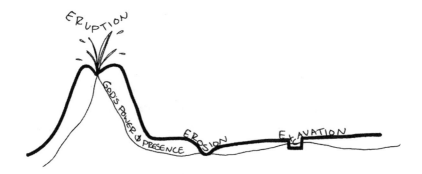

This book is not only a collection of nuggets I have mined and want to pass along, but is written in hopes that you will learn to be a miner, too. If you read and treat this simply as a collection of someone else's devotional thoughts and stop there, then I will have failed in what I hope to achieve. There's plenty more gold "down there." And my goal is to model the way until you learn to dig for yourself! (You know, teach a person to fish and ....) Again, I believe that if you excavate Scripture expectantly and with discipline, you will never be without the guidance of the Holy Spirit in very concrete ways that inform your life and leadership.

Audience

This book is for leaders. If you have formal or informal influence over another person, group, or situation, you are a leader. And you can benefit from turning to the Bible with an eye for what it has to say about leadership. I hope pastors and Bible teachers will be able to use this book, but even more, it is for managers, school teachers, bank tellers, students, CEOs and landscapers.

We look at the Old Testament period between Isaiah and Malachi because it is rife with examples of both the promise and failure of leaders. Legendary patriarchs are gone, current kings (even the great ones) and others in charge are failing in their spiritual stewardship. Those in official positions are often incompetent or wicked, teaching us that leadership never automatically proceeds from title. The entire period makes for a case study of the great good that can be done through effective leadership (even in dark times), as well as the costs of squandered leadership opportunities. In this sense, it is a treasure trove for leaders who want to learn on the dime of others and make good leadership calls today.

The great prophetic leaders are great listeners to God. My conviction is that, for Christians, leadership should be viewed through the lens of discipleship. The best leaders of people are the best followers of Jesus. The core work of leading is to listen to our Leader before we try to lead anyone else anywhere else."

Dallas Willard has repeatedly stated that the two most important questions we can ask of Christians today are, "What's your plan for discipleship?" and "How's that plan working?" If leaders are disciples, and leaders are planners, then this book is an attempt to help you map out strategically a plan for listening that is at the heart of great leadership. In Willard's teaching, you will have to "abstain" from some things in order to detach from their claims on your ear, mind, eye, and heart. Such *abstinence* then leads to time and space for disciplines of *engagement*, where we are free to truly hear and prepared to respond to God. God has a word worth hearing, and if you will learn to listen daily, it will help you with self-leadership and with leading others. This is how to optimize our opportunities and indeed our lives!

Methods

There are several ways to picture how we want to build this muscle for listening to God, leading others, and optimizing our lives. Here's one:

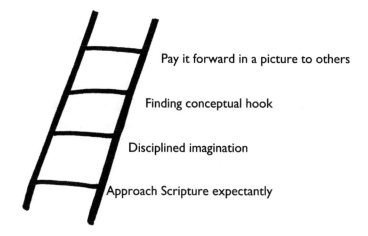

Pay it forward in a picture to others

Finding conceptual hook

Disciplined imagination

Approach Scripture expectantly

Here, we <u>plan</u> to come to the Bible every day out of confidence that it will be the most useful thing we can do as we prepare to lead. We come as part of the very rhythm of our life, like breakfast for our soul. Then, as we read with an eye for what God might say about leadership, we listen for a <u>hook</u>, a simple and straightforward word from God that emanates out of the characters, storyline, or direct teaching of the Scripture. Finally, as my friends in recovery say, "you can't keep it until you give it away." In other words, the leadership insights that come from the hook must be paid forward and passed along to someone else before they are fully activated in our own lives. Sharing what you have heard with someone else is the "activation code" or catalyst that brings the insight to life in leadership. Mastery comes through gifting to others.

I believe that the best way to do this is through a simple picture. Edward Tufte and Dan Roam have taught us that perhaps the best way to bring conceptual information to life and application is through simple, visual means. If you can't write it on the "back of a napkin," you haven't really absorbed the insight to the point where it is useful to you and others. Mike Breen, in using "LifeShapes," has understood this, and I have seen firsthand many times the power of a simple visual diagram to communicate vast leadership insights. Simple, visual information has the ability to be cross-cultural and multi-generational. It has the wherewithal to cut through the muck of words and get to the heart of action-oriented, mind-changing, behavior-modifying leadership.

Breen's triangle (of course) illustrates this:

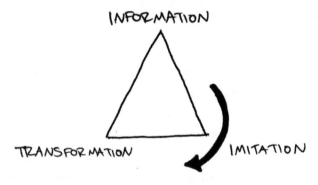

The great fallacy of how we grow is that we move straight from *Information* to *Transformation*. But "more informed" clearly does not automatically equate to "fully transformed." To get to *transformation*, one must first go through a process of *imitation*. We need models, mentors, demonstrations, living examples. We need people who can, step-by-step, show us how a word from God became part of our life, and how it can become a part of your life. This is why Paul repeatedly said to his young churches, *"Imitate me, just as I also imitate Christ"* (1 Corinthians 11:1). The Incarnation demonstrates that we need knowledge embodied, modeled, and lived out before it can become part of our way of being and doing. Only then does knowledge become wisdom and revelation:

Leadership (gained as we pay it forward by sketching it for another)

Wisdom/Revelation (gained as we capture the "hook," i.e. in a drawing)

Knowledge/Insight (gained as we engage with Scripture)

So, while God will impress upon us great insights while we engage with Scripture, those insights do not become a part of our transformation until we capture and then pass them along. And we can pass them along by sketching them out for another person to receive in such a way that they, too, can pay it forward.

Again, there are 929 chapters in the Old Testament and 250 in the books from Isaiah to Malachi. Choosing only 157 of those chapters, I have come nowhere close to exhausting the insights available even in those selected chapters. My aim is for this to be a how-to manual, not a coffee table book. Watch what I do here, and then imitate this habit in your own way. My hope is that you will learn to engage with Old Testament leaders in a way that informs the decisions you have to make every day as you lead people. My prayer is that, after practicing through this book, you will have built the muscles to do the work of mining on your own as you continue to excavate the Bible. I can promise that it will change you as a disciple and as a leader.

Operating Instructions: *How to use*

Before opening the Bible ...

Just do it. Begin the discipline of studying a chapter of the Bible a day on the very day you get this book. Don't procrastinate and don't try to wait until the beginning of a new book of the Bible or first day of the month or year.

Kneel. I suggest a beginning with a brief physical gesture, or ritual that will help you to put yourself in a posture of receiving. I use a kneeler bench outside of my bedroom door, so that before I walk out for the day, I have submitted to God for guidance. However you choose, ask God to open your heart to hearing as you submit yourself to the discipline of listening to the Bible.

Prepare your workspace. I find it very useful to have a certain desk where I do this work every day; it is part of a routine which helps form habit. It is a signal to my body and mind of what I am about to undertake. Bring with you a Bible you can write in, a pen, and a ruler. A notepad is useful for putting persistent distractions in a parking lot until later.

Plan. For me, writing key notes in a single Bible is useful. Working on a single chapter per day (or sometimes a slightly longer thought-unit) sets a consistent scope. Block off your daily calendar and notify those who need to know that you are unavailable during this time.

Win the first battle of the day. "Time" and "Space" are the media of creation in Genesis 1 and continue to be today. There will be a battle for your heart and for your attention. For me, I had to postpone reading two daily newspapers and discard *SportsCenter*. It will be vital to read the Bible before texts, email, Facebook, Twitter, etc. Turn the sound notifications off on all devices and resolve to open yourself to Scripture before engaging electronically.

While the Bible is open before you ...

Start with the Bible alone. Before looking at commentaries, annotations, or anything anyone else has said about the Scripture before you, give your chapter a chance to speak to you on its own terms. Read, re-read, and perhaps read aloud until you digest the chapter. I also practice by reading it in Spanish; if you know another language, use it to slow you down and think more richly about nuances.

Underline intuitively. When (re)reading the chapter of the day, highlight and underline intuitively. Where do words, phrases, sentences, verses, or even whole sections of Scripture jump off of the page at you? Don't over-think, but make notes of strong impressions.

Study alongside of church history. You can't know what the Bible means to me until you know what it meant to the people to whom it was written, and you can't know what the Bible meant until you actually listen to what it says. Beyond "impressionism" lays the rigorous examination of three thousand years of reflection by others who have engaged with the Bible. Pick a few trusted commentaries – and if you know don't whom to trust, ask someone who does – and let them serve as guides to help you listen to the Scripture. You don't want to do this *before* listening on your own to Scripture … but you don't want to be the only one listening to the Scripture. For me, heroes like Walter Brueggemann are trustworthy guides to hearing the Bible on its own terms. Read what one or two commentaries say about your chapter. Take notes where the insights of others illumine your reading so that if you were to go back later to a page of Scripture, ideas for the interpretation of that passage would be on the page and ready to share.

Hone in. Now, after having used the wide-angle lens, narrow it back down. From your own impressions and from the insights gained by wider study, hone in on one focal verse. (At times, it may be a single word, the action of a character, or a short passage. Don't get too legalistic about it.) By this point, your underlining and notes will be great clues.

Receive again. As you hone in on your verse, ask God to reveal what he is trying to say about how you lead and how you might help others lead. This is what I mean by reading the Bible through the lens of leadership, and leadership through the lens of discipleship. Ask for a "word" from God. Using the key verse, ask the Lord to fix in your mind and heart for the day some divine direction or guidance. It may be as simple as a single word that you want to repeat throughout the day. Or, it could be a phrase, the verse itself, or illustration of a key story of the biblical text. Ask God for grace to remember and return to that word throughout that day. This is not hocus-pocus but more akin to Paul Ricoeur's "second naiveté."

Praying the Prophets

After you have closed the Bible ...

Use "fresh bread." Before leaving the time and space of the "first battle of the day," commit to sharing in some venue (verbal or written) your received "word" from God (a verse/principle/story) during same day that you received it. Resolve to share what you have heard and learned with someone in a situation that will become apparent to you only once you are in it. Don't cram or force it, but go into the day open to sharing what you yourself have heard from Scripture and how it is affecting you. As often as not, you will be giving testimony as to how God is changing you as a leader as you will be offering input to someone else about how they lead.

Draw it on the back of a napkin. We close the loop when we pay forward to someone else what God has offered to us. Do so by sharing the word you have received with a very simple illustration or diagram. Such a picture gives you ways to "operationalize" insights into active leadership practice and make it useful in daily life. It will not only potentially help a person you are trying to lead; it will also finish the circuit for your own absorption of the word from God in your life.

ISAIAH 1

NO OBLIGATION TO LISTEN

"When you stretch out your hands, I will hide my eyes from you; even though you make many prayers, I will not listen ..."
– Isaiah 1:15

The first chapter of Isaiah introduces us to the Major Prophets (Isaiah, Jeremiah, Ezekiel) who address Judah, and the "Twelve" or Minor Prophets (Hosea though Malachi) who address Israel. The prophets present three dominant images of God: leader/King ("*Sovereign*"), Almighty of heaven and earth (*Lord of hosts*), and Holy One of Israel (v. 24). These presentations of God call into question all whose rituals have become only a hollow shell.

Chillingly, the core indictment by the prophets in general and Isaiah in particular is that God is not obligated to listen to his people. Just because the people engage in rituals of offerings (vv. 10-13), observances of seasons (vv. 13f), and fervent prayers (v. 15), God does not automatically respond. God is not a robot who springs to life when we push the right buttons. When our rituals (v. 16) are not matched by justice (v. 17), God turns a deaf ear.

Israel and Judah were prophetically chastised when they believed that they received a privileged hearing by virtue of their status as chosen people. And leaders who believe that people should listen to them simply because they have been designated as leaders will one day face a chilling reality otherwise. Position, title, or status doesn't grant us rights; integrity between words and actions do. We gain a hearing for our prayers when our deeds for justice correspond with our petitions.

ISAIAH 2

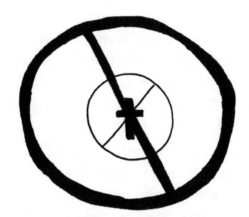

AGAINST BAD RELIGION

"... they shall beat their swords into plowshares, and their spears into pruning hooks; nation shall not lift up sword against nation, neither shall they learn war anymore."
— Isaiah 2:4

This opening prophetic salvo is also fired in Micah 4:3. As a "floating poem" it signals what every biblical prophet tries to provide: an alternative vision for human thriving. Prophets rail against a violent present by presenting a better future of *shalom*.

Much of what is wrong with the violent present can be traced to bad religion. Isaiah calls such idolatry "*treasures*" (v. 7); the Hebrew *elihim* ("wee gods") contrasts *Elohim*, the name of Israel's God. In three stanzas of 2:6-22, Isaiah says that idolatry is marked by superstition, materialism, and haughtiness. Because of bad religion, Judah has forgotten its identity and become like all the other nations.

There is nothing virtuous about "faith" and "devotion" and "prayer" per se. It all depends on the God to whom one's faith, devotion, and prayer is directed. Worship the wrong gods and you only get more "*swords*" and "*spears.*" But the God of the Bible moves history toward a vision of *shalom* and human flourishing. And every biblical prophet and prophetic leader today corrects the present toward that peaceful future.

Exercise: *Is the major challenge for you right now* superstition, materialism, *or* haughtiness *(pride)? How so? As you meditate on how this is expressed, ask God to drill down into your life to remove this defect of idolatry from you.*

ISAIAH 3-4

"Indeed over all the glory there will be a canopy. It will serve as a pavilion, a shade by day from the heat, and a refuge and a shelter from the storm and rain." – Isaiah 4:5-6

By chapter 3, the prophet Isaiah is in full swing, and his condemnation of unjust leaders who are "*crushing*" and "*grinding*" (3:15) their people is unsparing. Chapter 3 lists the removal of eleven (male-led) offices deemed vital for the continuity of the state. 3:16-4:1 lists twenty-one items of female adornment taken away from women. Whether one finds their identity in work, position, or appearance, the unjust will reap the disgrace they have sown. Male and female, they are leaders who have failed, and their failure has turned on them in full force.

God, however, has provided a *branch* (4:2), a remnant "*recorded for life*" *(v.* 3), an "*assembly*" covered by a "*canopy or pavilion over all the glory.*" This community is a "*refuge*" and "*shelter from the storm and rain.*" Here are men and women who live well in the world and rightly use their resources for the well-being of all.

We interpret Isaiah as describing the church here, the people of God. At our best, we are an alternative community that stands in judgment of leaders who crush the poor and who take advantage of position of privilege. We are a contrast society that pre-figures the final "setting right of all things" that God promises. This is the way God is drawing all of creation to a close. When the world wants to see what is coming, they should look to the church as the embodiment of the divine justice, the living demonstration of the *shalom* of God.

Exercise: *Am I, in any undue way, overweighting my* <u>work/position</u> *or my* <u>appearance</u>? *If so, what is one way that I can reboot that sense of self through connecting more deeply with the church community? Resolve to deepen those ties and meditate on how to do so, both today and this week.*

ISAIAH 5

"And now I will tell you what I will do to my vineyard. I will remove its hedge, and it shall be devoured; I will break down its wall, and it shall be trampled down."
– Isaiah 5:5

Isaiah 5 is a prophetic oracle in judgment against Israel and Judah. Delivered at a "vintage celebration" (the harvest festival of booths), the prophet rails judgment against a very smug (and surprised) people. They came for a drinking party and got a two-by-four instead!

What is instructive is how Isaiah delivers his broadside. He uses a vineyard parable (5:1-7), much in the tradition of Hosea 1-2 or Nathan (2 Samuel 12:1-12). He follows this parable with a series of six "woes": against insensitive accumulation (vv. 8f), carousing (vv. 11f), mockery (vv. 18f), twisting the truth (vv. 20f), conceited pride (v. 21), and drunken bravado in bribery (vv. 22f). Thus Isaiah delivers a surprisingly hard word by indirect, and then very direct means. Jesus would later confront in much the same way (compare his parable in Matthew 20 with his "woes" in Matthew 23).

By definition, a leader often has to confront. Prophetic judgment often trumps popularity in polls. The artful leader can take cues from the prophet Isaiah. Sometimes mandates must be delivered in a parabola, an arc, through the back door. Sometimes only very blunt confrontation will do. Good leaders know when to use indirect parables and when to speak direct woes. They tailor their approach toward whatever will gain the hearing that leads to change.

ISAIAH 6

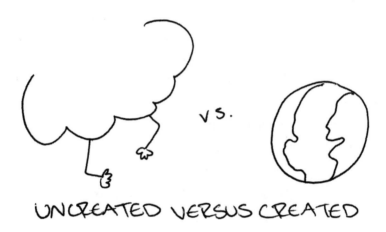

UNCREATED VERSUS CREATED

"Holy, holy, holy is the Lord of hosts; the whole earth is full of his glory." – Isaiah 6:3

The late preacher John Claypool often taught that the Bible indicates two fundamental orders of reality: the *Uncreated*, which has life in itself and is self-sufficient. And, the *created*, which derives its life and power from the generosity of the Uncreated. Everything *except* God belongs on the created side of the line. Nothing *but* God belongs in the realm of the uncreated. The great awareness that came to Isaiah is that God is in a realm all by himself. There is nothing comparable of God. God is "*holy, holy, holy.*"

Isaiah's experience of "call" is a signal that you and I are to ascribe a kind of reverence, fear, adoration, awe, or worship to the Uncreated and holy God that we never give to *anything* in the created realm. Because if we treat anything that is created as if it were the Uncreated, then we are committing the sin that the Bible calls, *idolatry* – which is ruinous to us and those around us. Like a swimming instructor says, "You've got to respect the water. It can hold you up and give you great delight. It can also drown you. It's not your choice how to relate to the water. You have to relate to water on water's terms." So it is with how we relate to the Uncreated.

Our call as leaders comes from a holy God. Our call is God's idea, not ours. It sends us to hard places with difficult words. The good news for us is that our call and its effects do not depend on our creativity, but on that of the Uncreated One!

ISAIAH 8

PROPER FEAR

*"Do not call conspiracy all that this people calls conspiracy,
and do not fear what it fears, or be in dread. But the Lord of
hosts, him you shall regard as holy; let him be your fear and
let him be your dread. He will become a sanctuary, a stone
one strikes against." – Isaiah 8:12-14*

On a tour of the Louisville Slugger bat factory, I once asked the fifth-generation leader of the company, Jack Hillerich, about what worried him most. I anticipated his answer to be about how difficult it is to innovate in a tradition-rich company and sport like baseball. But his blunt answer was that he feared "the competition." When Nike or Adidas can throw millions on a product line, even a fifth-generation business can be gone tomorrow.

Isaiah prophesies against improper fear. A superstitious, jittery people attuned to every political machination of king-in-name Ahaz is warned that their fear is misplaced. Fear a holy God instead, says the prophet. In recalibrating what you are afraid of, you will then, says Isaiah, find a fearsome God to be a "*sanctuary*" and as solid as an anvil, "*a stone one strikes against.*"

The role of the prophetic leader is to recalibrate the fear of those s/he leads. Jim Collins writes of "productive paranoia" as a core component of companies who would be *Great by Choice*. The message is not to have zero fear; the message is to have proper fears. Superstition is counterproductive. Proper fear leads one to trust in a solid God who can deliver even in the most dicey situations.

Exercise: *Name one proper fear and one improper fear that is part of your life right now. As these come into focus, ask God to rebalance what gets attention in your heart and mind throughout the day.*

ISAIAH 9

"*For a child is born for us, a son given to us; authority rests on his shoulder; and he is named Wonderful Counselor, Mighty God, Everlasting Father, Prince of Peace.*"
– Isaiah 9:6

Isaiah 9 was read by Robert Frost at John F. Kennedy's inauguration as our nation looked toward the ideal of "president." In much the same way, the eighth-century prophet looked toward king Hezekiah as God's answer to the prayers of oppressed people. Since then, Christians have declared that this *"child born for us"* and *"son given to us"* is fulfilled in Jesus Christ. In all of these messianic prayers, people are looking for an experience of <u>hope</u>.

How then does hope come? In what form does the God who gives hope make himself known? Isaiah suggests four:

- ☙ **"Wonderful counselor"** – *"wonderful"* signifies "not of this world," the Guide who makes known to us wisdom and the path we should take;

- ☙ **"Mighty God"** – victorious hero, conquering warrior, the Leader who gives us triumph;

- ☙ **"Everlasting Father"** – persevering, steadfast, and faithful, our heavenly Father (1:2) who looks upon us and looks out for us forever; and

- ☙ **"Prince of Peace"** – giver of shalom who *"is our peace; in his flesh he has made both groups into one and has broken down the dividing wall, that is, the hostility between us"* (Ephesians 2:14).

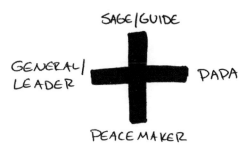

We who lead can look to the God of the Bible and signal hope for our people by identifying which of these four expressions of God best fit the needs of those we lead. Do they need a sage? A general? Papa? A peacemaker? Our God is the finest and fullest expression of each of these. Leaders first follow such a magnificent God, and then point our people to the God who fulfills each longing for hope.

Exercise: *Which of the four images of God in Isaiah 9 would give you the most hope right now? Spend a few minutes praising God for being (your image) to you and to the world.*

ISAIAH 10

INSTRUMENTS, NOT PLAYERS

"Shall the ax vaunt itself over the one you wields it, or the saw magnify itself against the one who handles it? As if a rod should raise the one who lifts it up, or as if a staff should lift the one who is not wood!" – Isaiah 10:15

Praying the Prophets

After describing Assyria as God's means of judging unfaithful Israel, Isaiah 10 then speaks truth to power by condemning Assyria for its blasphemous hubris. Blasphemy means boldly reversing the relationship between the Creator and any created thing. The leaders of Assyria have assumed that, because they were <u>currently</u> in power, they were <u>ultimately</u> in power. Bad move. Isaiah lets them know that they will soon enough get what's coming to them. We will all find out one day who is Creator!

Blasphemous power-brokers are marked by "*arrogant boasting and haughty pride*" (v. 12). They are fundamentally confused, thinking themselves as <u>wielders</u> of power (as an "*ax* or *rod* or *staff*") rather than as <u>instruments</u> of power in the hands of the Lord. Because of this, God will lay waste to them like a fire (vv. 16-19).

As a leader, when you think you are the player of the instrument rather than an instrument through which God plays, you are on some thin ice! For this reason, the prayer of Saint Francis of Assisi has been a great help to leaders who wish to remember humility, teachability, and servanthood as their primary charge:

> "Lord, make me an **instrument of your peace**.
> Where there is hatred, let me sow love.
> Where there is injury, pardon.
> Where there is doubt, faith.
> Where there is despair, hope.
> Where there is darkness, light.
> Where there is sadness, joy.
> O Divine Master,
> grant that I may not so much seek to be consoled, as to console;
> to be understood, as to understand;
> to be loved, as to love.
> For it is in giving that we receive.
> It is in pardoning that we are pardoned,
> and it is in dying that we are born to Eternal Life.
> Amen."

John P. Chandler

ISAIAH 11

WISDOM AND HOPE

"On that day the root of Jesse shall stand as a signal to all the peoples; the nations shall inquire of him, and his dwelling shall be glorious." – Isaiah 11:10

Again, Isaiah speaks to a "deforested" people by offering a hopeful picture of a "*shoot*" coming out of a "*stump*" (v. 1). This messianic king (Hezekiah? Josiah? Jesus?) is the embodiment of a well-led people, so that they become a "*signal*" from God to the world to the *shalom* intended for all creation. In this world to come (vv. 6-9), the wolf, leopard, lion, bear, serpent live in harmony with lamb/kid/calf/child – all tribes are in harmony; indeed, all of creation! Chaos (the raging "*sea*" and "*river*" of v. 15) is tamed by the well-led people of God.

This ideal leader is marked by a deft combination of "*spirit*" (mentioned four times in vv. 2ff) and "*wisdom/reason/justice/righteousness*." The messiah will thus not only be able to project a hopeful vision of a brighter day to come, but also to rule (like Solomon in 1 Kings 3) with soundness in day-to-day matters.

In the words of the great hymn, "*Great is Thy Faithfulness*," such a leader points and mimics the Messiah's work of providing "strength for today and bright hope for tomorrow." Adept leaders do their work by signaling both wisdom and hope.

ISAIAH 12

"With joy you will draw water from the wells of salvation."
– Isaiah 12:3

Praying the Prophets

Isaiah has pronounced God's judgment on Israel at the hands of Assyria, and then on the Assyrians for their pride. The prophet then offers a sign of hope (9:6ff, 11:1ff), a coming messiah/king, who will lead the nation like a shoot sprouting out of a burned-out stump. Chapter 12 then names the song of deliverance God's people will sing after the Lord does this work.

There is always a new song we sing after God delivers. Miriam takes up the tambourine after the Red Sea parts (Exodus 15:20f). Mary sings after the conception of Jesus (Luke 1:46-55). The prodigal returns home to music and dancing (Luke 15:25). God never simply leads people out of misery; from there, he leads us into a party with singing! Isaiah's picture of that party imagines the ability to *"draw water from the wells of salvation"* and to do so with *"joy."* Ease of access to water in an arid culture is cause for a celebration, indeed. Jesus would later tell a woman at a well of such a hopeful future (John 4:14).

We do not lead by merely painting a picture of escape or exodus from a miserable present. Isaiah portrays a coming time when *"great in your midst is the Holy One of Israel"* (v. 6), water coming to us with happy ease. It is an imaginative song of a hopeful future.

You cannot lead simply by describing an intolerable present condition. Unless and until we can compose such a tune of future hope toward which we are leaning, we are not leading.

Exercise: *In what way are you focused on escape from something and need to be reframed toward a hopeful future instead? Pray that God will today give you a picture of the Promised Land in which you might dwell and not just the Exodus from where you are currently.*

ISAIAH 13

BEYOND COMPETITION

"I will punish the world for its evil, and the wicked for their iniquity; I will put an end to the pride of the arrogant, and lay low the insolence of tyrants." – Isaiah 13:11

Isaiah 13 begins a long section of the book (chapters 13-23) focused on God's judgment on the nations and their gods. The God of the Bible is not simply one god among many, another local deity. God is "*Lord of hosts*" (v. 4), in the phrase of theologian Paul Tillich, "the God above all gods." God is of a different order altogether, and his purposes transcend merely outmuscling rivals who on nearly-equal footing. In fact, the prophet boldly claims that even the kings and gods of other nations oppressing Israel (i.e. the Babylonians or Assyrians) are mere obedient soldiers mustered by the Commander of all.

A vision organized principally around besting the competition has limited power to transform. Roberto Goizueta, famous former CEO of Coca Cola, transformed the company when he declared that Coke's competition was not Pepsi, but tea, milk, and water. "We are looking not for victory in the cola wars," he said, "but for a share of the human stomach." The oppressed Israelites needed to hear more than the hope that they, too, would one day have their day in the sun. Hope finally comes not in besting our rivals, but in the broader vision of a God above gods and Kingdom above kingdoms.

Leaders do well to remember that our best messages don't stop with declaring that "we are one step ahead of our rivals." Rather, there are righteous causes that are beyond competition, right of their own sake. Competition may be necessary, but it is never sufficient. Leaders must give voice to a vision of transformation. And those who follow the God of the Bible know that such a vision comes from the transcendent God.

ISAIAH 14

ARROGANT KINGS FALL

*"How you are fallen from heaven, O Day Star, son of Dawn!
How you are cut down to the ground, you who laid the
nations low! You said in your heart, "I will ascend to heaven;
I will raise my throne above the stars of God ... But you are
brought down to Sheol, to the depths of the Pit."*
— Isaiah 14:12-15

This chapter is part of a long soliloquy of oracles against the nations and rulers who have taken turns oppressing the people of God. It is a future picture of the vindication of God, which might be summarized by the phrase, "How the mighty have fallen!" Noteworthy is Isaiah's unblinking declaration of God's judgment of arrogant kings. These royal leaders (Babylonian, Assyrian, Philistine, etc.) de-forest the land to build their palaces (v. 8). They write pompous music for themselves (v. 11). Gallingly, their aspirations are divine, as reflected by the titles they use for themselves ("*Day Star, son of Dawn,*" mythological Canaanite deities).

But Isaiah declares that every king comes under the final judgment of God. Rulers who have Babel-like hopes to "*ascend to heaven*" will be "*broken*" (v. 5), "*struck down with unceasing blows*" (v. 6), and sleep in a final bed of "*maggots and worms*" (v. 11). No wonder that this arrogant song of the Babylonian king (Nebuchadnezzar) was later used by Jesus to describe the fall of Satan himself (Luke 10:15-20) and by Paul to describe the antichrist (2 Thessalonians 2:4).

We tend to judge actions, not people. But as Indonesian scholar S.H. Widyapranawa writes, "The modern evangelist who declares that God loves "you" but hates your sins is out of tune with the biblical revelation. For Isaiah it is the sinner, not his sins, who is under the judgment of the God of love."

No leader escapes final personal accountability. No matter our current power or influence, we will all answer to the watchful Almighty. The leader who arrogantly forgets this will experience the warning of Proverbs 16:18: "*Pride goes before destruction, and a haughty spirit before a fall.*"

John P. Chandler 45

ISAIAH 16

WEEPING FOR
YOUR ENEMIES

"Therefore my heart throbs like a harp for Moab ..."
– Isaiah 16:11

Isaiah 15-16 is a lament (!) for the downfall of one of Israel's traditional enemies. The prophet does not withhold the truth – Moab has been undone by their own *"arrogance, pride, insolence and boasts"* (16:6). These cost Moab an opportunity for refuge, sanctuary, asylum; they always do. But rather than relish the downfall of an enemy (like Jonah did), Isaiah mourns the fate of Moab. In the opening verses of lament, nine places are mentioned with six verbs for weeping; Moab is totally undone, and the people of God weep for their fallen rival.

Moab famously refused Israel hospitality when Israel wandered from Egypt through the desert (Deuteronomy 2:26ff). But Isaiah doesn't return hate for hate. He wishes the *"lambs/nestlings/daughters/outcasts/fugitives"* of Moab could find *"shade like night at the height of noon"* in the *"refuge"* of Judah's sanctuary (16:1-4). This is a hospitality which goes beyond merely reciprocate an earlier favor.

It is one thing to weep, as the prophet Jeremiah did, for the downfall of your own people. But it is quite another to lament the undoing of one's enemy. Abraham prayed for the sparing of Sodom and Gomorrah (Genesis 18:16ff) and Jesus wept for salvation of the Jerusalem that would soon kill him (Luke 13:33f).

In this same vein, Isaiah shows us that prophets must give their warnings not with a vengeful sneer of "You'll get yours!", but with tears. The vision of a hopeful kingdom to be *"established in steadfast love in the tent of David,"* ruled by a leader who is full of *"faithfulness,"* *"justice,"* and who is *"swift to do what is right"* (v. 5) is big enough even to include one's enemies.

John P. Chandler   47

ISAIAH 22

"The Lord is about to hurl you away violently, my fellow. He will seize firm hold on you, whirl you round and round, and throw you like a ball into a wide land; there you will die, and there your splendid chariots shall lie, O you disgrace to your master's house!" – Isaiah 22:17-18

Isaiah 22 is a warning against two besetting temptations of every leader: <u>complacency</u> and <u>arrogance</u>. Arrogance is defined as holding power but failing to *"look to him or did it, or have regard for him who planned it long ago"* (v. 11).

Complacency is given more attention by describing the fate of Shebna, who is described as *"master of the household"* (v. 15). Literally, this immigrant high official is a <u>steward</u>, a person in high power during national crisis. But he has not used his stewardship properly, instead being concerned first with a prestigious burial/tomb/monument for himself (v. 16), and using the national *"chariots"* (power) for his own gain. Bluntly, the prophet says the Lord will ball Shebna up and throw him in the trash. He is a *"disgrace to his master's house."*

As preacher Andy Stanley has famously said, leadership is stewardship, and the leader is accountable. We are accountable to the visibility and power of our position. We have fewer rights and less leeway than most. And woe to any who forgets this and misuses the platform entrusted by God to them.

Exercise: *Is your greater danger today <u>complacency</u> or <u>arrogance</u>? Ask God for help in dealing with your current besetting temptation. Pray to be a better steward of what is currently in your charge.*

ISAIAH 23

"At the end of seventy years, the Lord will visit Tyre, and she will return to her trade, and will prostitute herself with all the kingdoms of the world on the face of the earth. Her merchandise and her wages will be dedicated to the Lord; her profits will not be stored or hoarded, but her merchandise will supply abundant food and fine clothing for those who live in the presence of the Lord." – Isaiah 23:17-18

This arresting image caps Isaiah's long series of judgments against the nations (chapters 13-23). It is a woe to Sidon, the flavor-of-the-month most powerful economy in the world and commercial center of the Near East. The prophet warns Sidon that her wealth will not protect her from the judgment of God. Despite her current prosperity, she will soon wail like a ghost ship or barren woman (vv. 1-4) when God reminds her who is truly in charge.

Such warnings are common in the Bible. No matter which empire is currently in vogue in human history, the kingdoms of this world will always eventually be subject to the true King of this world. Any king or nation which ignores this reality does so at their own peril.

What is uncommon is Isaiah's striking picture of the restoration of a once-fallen economic engine. Like a *"forgotten prostitute"* (v. 16) now *"remembered,"* Isaiah envisions a time when even the unlovely and fallen will be restored by the divine King. Even a prostitute's wages will be *"dedicated to the Lord,"* not *"stored or hoarded,"* and will *"supply food and fine clothing"* for others. Even shady commerce itself will be redeemed, so that a nation's economy, once driven by greed, envy, and lust, will now function for the well-being of communities and *shalom* of the nation. Any leader who works to redeem economies so that they build community is working in harmony with the final work of God.

Will God judge powerful nations? Undoubtedly. Is God able to redeem anyone and even seamy economies to transform into a beloved community? O, with Isaiah, let us pray that it will be so!

ISAIAH 24

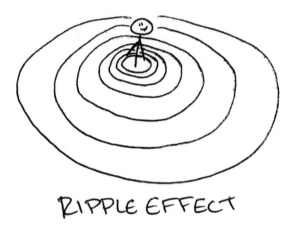

RIPPLE EFFECT

"The earth lies polluted under its inhabitants; for they have transgressed laws, violated the statues, broken the everlasting covenant." – **Isaiah 24:5**

Chapters 24-27 are called the "Isaiah Apocalypse." They speak as cosmically as the opening chapters of Genesis and closing chapters of Revelation. Beyond whatever "flavor of the month" empire is in charge now, God spoke creation into being and will bring it to a close. Isaiah 24 does what the Bible so often does: it employs poetic language to describe the certainty of God's sovereign and final judgment.

A *"polluted"* earth will not be judged simply on account of general wickedness. Isaiah says that the greater fault lies with the failure of God's people and their leaders. It is covenant leaders (more than the heathen generally) who have *"transgressed laws, violated statutes, broken covenant."* When God's covenant people fail, creation pays. When God's leaders don't lead, the whole earth flames out spectacularly.

Jesus would later say, *"To whom much is given, much will be required"* (Luke 12:48). Good or bad, more is expected of covenant leaders. Leadership has a ripple effect, and Isaiah 24 describes it as a cosmic effect.

What response is called for? Isaiah's *"flood"* language (v. 18) echoes Noah as a signal to Isaiah's hoped-for response. Godly leaders, like Noah (Genesis 6-8), are willing to act and lead counter to the prevailing culture and powers-that-be. They build an ark while others mock. They preserve creation in the face of its imminent destruction. They listen to God and not the clamoring masses.

True of Noah, true of Isaiah's time, true of today! When leaders don't lead with the courage of Noah, chaos and pollution ensue. When they do, a remnant preserves the hope of God for the redemption of the earth.

ISAIAH 26

"Those of steadfast mind you keep in peace – in peace because they trust in you." – Isaiah 26:3

In "Isaiah's Apocalypse" (Isaiah 24-27), the prophet draws sweeping conclusions. Surveying two hundred years of Israel's experience with hostile empires (Assyria and Babylon), the prophet takes the long view of what God is doing with his chosen people. The conclusions are announced in poetic form: God is about to destroy the serpent, a new vineyard will soon emerge, all will be invited on a straight path to a glorious banquet in this new upside-down reign of peace.

Because of this framework, leaders can have a *"steadfast mind"* and can experience the *"peace"* that comes with *"trust"* in God. James 1:6 would later describe this as a wise faith unavailable to the doubter who is *"like a wave of the sea, driven and tossed by the wind, double-*minded." This *"peace/trust"* is a state of steadfastness, confidence, and fixedness that never trades quarterly results for long-term profitability.

In this long view, the prophet warns leaders not to trust in short term foreign alliances, false friends, or nations who overpromise and under-deliver. Lie down with dogs, and you will eventually wake up with fleas.

Wise leaders are circumspect about leaning on seasonal, dicey allies. Instead, they trust finally in a God who finally governs the long and certain sweep of human history.

Exercise: *Is there a "false friend" in my life? If so, how is my trust in this person or entity displacing more well-placed trust in God? Ask God for a more steady and peaceful heart as you root out unreliable sources for confidence.*

ISAIAH 28

"... therefore thus says the Lord God, See, I am laying in Zion a foundation stone, a tested stone, a precious cornerstone, a sure foundation: One who trusts will not panic."
– Isaiah 28:16

Isaiah 28-35 is a collection of six "woes" against arrogant leaders who mock Isaiah and the purposes of God. In chapter 28, the mocking leaders are priests (vv. 7-13) and public scoffers (vv. 14f) who deride Isaiah as boring and superficial. They claim that Isaiah speaks only "*precept upon precept, line upon line, here a little, there a little.*" Isaiah lets them know that they will hear gibberish soon enough: the alien language of foreign conquerors who pounce upon their drunken dissipation and inattention as leaders.

But a better leader is coming, says Isaiah. This leader, like a wise farmer (vv. 23-29), interprets well the actions of God's plowing, leveling, threshing, etc. This leader is like a "*foundation cornerstone,*" a plumb and solid base upon which one can build. This image is later frequently used of Jesus Christ as the rock of the church (Matthew 16:16f, Ephesians 2:20, 1 Peter 2:4).

The neglected but critical image Isaiah uses of the leader, though, is that s/he is a "*tested stone*" (v. 16) or "touchstone." A touchstone is semi-precious, dark material (such as slate) used in antiquity to determine the purity and worth of gold and silver. Appearances can deceive, but touchstones ignite chemical reactions that unmask alloys. Metaphorically, Shakespeare (*As You Like It*) and others have written of touchstone characters as a sort of acid or litmus test.

A leader is a touchstone. The leader is not important than the mission s/he leads. The leader's worth is not intrinsic but is found in the service of testing or revealing truth and falsehood in service of what is precious.

Woe to the arrogant leader who places self above mission! And blessed is the leader who, in self-giving service, boldly calls out impurity and falsehood, and plainly points to a divine work greater than any one person.

John P. Chandler 57

ISAIAH 30

THE ANTI-LEADER

"For they are a rebellious people, faithless children, children who will not hear the instruction of the Lord; who say to the seers, "Do not see"; and to the prophets, "Do not prophesy to us what is right; speak to us smooth things, prophesy illusions, leave the way, turn aside from the path, Let us hear no more about the Holy One of Israel." – Isaiah 30:9-11

Isaiah 30 is one of six "woes" written to the nations. It is a fiery blast at Israel and her leaders, who should know better than to rely on Egypt (instead of God) as a defense against attacking Assyria. While it is not a treatise on leadership *per se*, it can be used as a warning for those who are in power, as it details the mistakes of leadership decisions in Israel around 703 B.C.

Here is some of what bad leaders do:

- ཀ They are like "*rebellious children*" (v. 1) – people who know better but who, in immaturity, do what they want anyway.

- ཀ They "*carry out a plan, but not mine*" – the criticism is not for lack of planning, but for scheming.

- ཀ They "*make an alliance, but against my will*" – picking the wrong advisors and counselors (v. 2).

- ཀ They silence the voices of "*prophets*" and "*seers*" who dissent (v. 10), preferring "*smooth talk*" and "*illusions.*"

- ཀ They trust in "*oppression and deceit*" (v. 12), relying on "*horses*" and "*steeds*" (v. 16) – the classic ancient symbols of human self-reliance in opposition to trust in God.

- ཀ They are surrounded by noise and motion, resisting the strength that comes from "*rest*" and "*quiet*" (v. 15).

Barbara Kellerman's book, *Bad Leadership*, details case studies of bad leaders. She argues that bad leaders can be corrupt, rigid, intemperate, callous, corrupt, insular, or evil. She may as well have gotten this list from Isaiah 30. The people of God are called to watch and learn from the mistakes of anti-leaders.

Exercise: *Can you identify a current bad leader? More than simply criticizing this person, ask what it is about his or her poor leadership that needs to serve as a correction or warning to you.*

ISAIAH 32

HORSES VERSUS SPIRIT

"… until a spirit from on high is poured out on us, and the wilderness becomes a fruitful field, and the fruitful field is deemed a forest. Then justice will dwell in the wilderness, and righteousness will abide in the fruitful field. The effect of righteousness will be peace, and the result of righteousness, quietness and trust forever." **– Isaiah 32:15-17**

Isaiah 32 is a visionary interlude in the middle of six "woes" against leaders who trust in *"horses"* (30:16, 31:1). Leaders within and outside of Israel have trusted in power to deliver them from their enemies – and they will be sorely disappointed. This interlude longs for a king, a messiah, who would lead differently. The fundamental difference would be seen in a new leader's reliance on the *"spirit from on high (which) is poured out on us,"* in contrast to trust in human horsepower.

This spirit can transform the natural order of things – *"wilderness"* becomes *"fruitful field,"* and field become lush *"forest."* The spirit is *"poured out"* like water. (In other places in the Bible, the spirit is like *"wind"* or *"fire"* – Acts 2:3. It is, in every image, elemental.) The marks of spirit-led leadership on the people are transformational: *"righteousness ... peace ... quietness ... trust ... secure ... rest."* Anxious warriors become serene farmers of fruitful land (v. 20).

What is a spirit-led leader? Among the many things the Bible says about this, Isaiah 32 highlights these:

1. This leader does not primarily rely on force and power (horses) to get things done. A prophetic vision of a better community is the spur to action.

2. S/he is dependent on God to *"pour out"* for a kind of transformation that can only be given from *"on high."* It is not achieved by human scheming or striving.

3. The outcome of his or her leadership is a habitation of *shalom,* a fruitful place of blessedness. Those who live in this community find fertility and justice.

4. The leader in Isaiah 32 is never named – because the outcome of a harmonious community is more important than the charismatic ego of the leader.

Prayer: *God of shalom, help me to be a Spirit-led leader. Teach me to rely on you and not my own horsepower. Don't let my ego get in the way. Give me a vision for a better community, a fruitful world of shalom where people, nature, and you are in harmony. Help me to lead out of quiet and rest, justice and righteousness, vision and trust. In the name of Jesus, Amen.*

ISAIAH 33

WHO CAN LIVE WITH FIRE?

"The sinners in Zion are afraid; trembling has seized the godless; who among us can live with the devouring fire? Who among us can live with everlasting flames?" – Isaiah 33:14

Isaiah speaks not of the fires of hell, but of the fires of heaven. God is a fire. God is a bush blazing but not consumed (Exodus 3:2f). God is a pillar of fire that leads his people through the wilderness at night (Exodus 13:21). God is a righteous fire that devours the wicked like stubble (Numbers 11:1) but refines the righteous like gold (Malachi 3:2, 1 Corinthians 3:13).

Who can live near such a fire? Both the people of God who are impure ("*sinners in Zion*") <u>and</u> people far from God ("*the godless*") will one day tremble before such a question.

Isaiah answers the question by listing six short requirements (v. 15). Each deals with interpersonal relationships. We can live near the fire of God when we:

1. "*Walk righteously,*"
2. "*Speak uprightly,*"
3. "*Despise the gain of oppression,*"
4. "*Wave away a bribe instead of accepting it,*"
5. "*Stop (our) ears from hearing of bloodshed,*" and
6. "*Shut (our) eyes from looking on evil.*"

The prophet's list is much like the second half of the Ten Commandments (Exodus 20:12ff), which also deals with social relationships (honor parents, don't murder or commit adultery, don't steal, lie, or covet). Live and speak well, don't be bought, and do not tolerate seeing or hearing that which does violence to others – do these things, Isaiah says, and holy fire will purify you instead of destroying you.

For leaders, beyond living well in the eyes of others, and beyond being able to look at ourselves in the mirror with a clear conscience, we are responsible to the "*everlasting flames*" of God which destroy or purify, consume or refine the deeds of every person.

John P. Chandler   65

ISAIAH 35

A HIGHWAY SHALL BE THERE

"A highway shall be there, and it shall be called the Holy Way; the unclean shall not travel on it, but it shall be for God's people; no traveler, not even fools, shall go astray."
– Isaiah 35:8

Isaiah 34-35, at the halftime of the prophet's message, provides a sweeping, symbolic interpretation of God's final work of destruction (chapter 34) and restoration (chapter 35). All of human history will be caught up in the sure and certain destruction of *"Edom"* (chapter 34, Esau, those who have intentionally rejected God for a bowl of soup; see Genesis 25:31ff), and the restoration of *"Zion"* (chapter 35, the restored paradise and city of God). Isaiah uses apocalyptic language because the final course of history will not be determined by whatever nation happens to be in charge at the time, but by the hand of the God who reigns over and above human history.

Isaiah's imagery of the final restoration of God for his people borrows from three sources:

1. The restoration of Eden (35:1f);

2. The healing of broken humanity (35:2-6); and

3. The Exodus road to the Promised Land (35:6-10).

Particularly beautiful is the promise of a *"highway"* or *"Holy Way"* through the desert. It will be the straight path (Proverbs 3:6) given by God, the beautiful road to the paradise God intends for those who know and love him. Neither the *"unclean"* nor *"any ravenous beast"* (vv. 8f) will travel this path. But those who love God and yet were "weak … feeble … blind … deaf … lame … fools" (vv. 3-6, 8) – these shall be restored and walk well on that *"highway"* to find final joy.

Leaders should take note of how Isaiah speaks God's clear judgment on the wicked and hope for the righteous: by presenting the *"Holy Way"* or path of God. It is no accident that Jesus would later call himself *"the Way"* (John 14:6). People are inspired when they know the way from where they are to where they will be going. People move when they know the steps. Leaders serve by highlighting the highway so that others may walk that path to restoration.

John P. Chandler

ISAIAH 36

THE TACTICS OF FALSE PROPHETS

"Do you think that mere words are strategy and power for war? On whom do you now rely, that you have rebelled against me?" – Isaiah 36:5

Praying the Prophets

Isaiah 36 is the record of the threat of the Rabshekah (field commander of the king of Assyria) against the righteous king of Judah, Hezekiah. The Rabshekah mocks Hezekiah's resistance to the Assyrians as *"mere words."* Yet it is ironically words/speech that the Rabshekah uses in an attempt to demoralize and discredit Hezekiah's leadership. Whoever said "Sticks and stones may break my bones, but names will never hurt me" was dead wrong. Words are powerful!

It can valuable for leaders to study the tactics of persuasion and intimidation in the Rabshekah's speech – both as a warning against using this kind of speech ourselves, and in debunking the attempts of enemies to demoralize us. Briefly, here is how this false prophet uses words to harm:

1. Insult – he refuses to address king Hezekiah by his royal title, treating him as a commoner (vv. 4, 14).

2. Dismissal – he waves off Hezekiah's strategy as ridiculous (vv. 4-6).

3. Twisting theology – the propagandist takes two tenets of Hezekiah's core beliefs (worshiping at one altar in Jerusalem, v. 6, and the providence of God, v. 10), and misuses them out of context to give a message exactly the opposite that those beliefs intend.

4. Rabble-rousing – foregoing diplomatic language, the Rabshekah now incites the crowd by a populist appeal to undermine the leadership of Hezekiah (vv. 13ff).

5. False promises – playing on the fears of the people, he offers a false Promised Land and false hope (vv. 16ff).

John P. Chandler

Words are mighty things. While the promises of false prophets are false, their tactics can be powerful. In the hands of the wrong leader who has the wrong bully pulpit, words can do great harm.

Exercise: *Is there any way that you are wrongly manipulating those whom you lead with false speech? If so, study the five false tactics of Isaiah 36 and identify where you are most prone to slip. Repent, and ask God to make you mindful of how you speak today.*

ISAIAH 37

WISE RESPONSE TO CRISIS

"Hezekiah received the letter from the hand of the messengers and read it; then Hezekiah went up to the house of the Lord and spread it before the Lord."
– Isaiah 37:14

King Hezekiah is a faithful leader facing a national crisis – impending attack from a fearsome national enemy. His response to the crisis precipitated by the aggression of Assyrian leaders is a model of wise leadership response to crisis. Here's how Hezekiah led when threatened:

1. Initial silence: *"the king's command was, "Do not answer him"* (36:21). Hezekiah did not escalate tensions by responding reflexively to intimidation and aggression.

2. Personal grief and repentance: *"When King Hezekiah heard it, he tore his clothes, covered himself with sackcloth ..."* (v. 1a). The leader did not show false bravado but acknowledged his need for help – especially for divine help.

3. Putting himself in a place where he could receive revelation: *"(he) went into the house of the Lord"* (v. 1b). Rather than scrambling feverishly, he short-circuited personal/national panic by stepping back from the urgent to put himself in a place (the temple) where he could take the long view.

4. Asking for the right people to help: *"the servants of King Hezekiah came to Isaiah ..."* (v. 5). He didn't respond simply out of his own ingenuity, but partnered with the prophet Isaiah. Prophet + King = a team capable of a mighty response to evil.

5. Openly asking God for divine intervention: *"Hezekiah ... spread it before the Lord. And Hezekiah prayed to the Lord ..."* (vv. 14f). The national king personally and publically acknowledged God as true King of all nations.

6. Mission before ego: *"O Lord our God, save us from his hand,*

so that all the kingdoms of the earth may know that you alone are the Lord" (v. 20). Ultimately, Hezekiah asked God to respond for the sake of God's purposes in the world, not for a narrow national agenda or personal aggrandizement.

God responded powerfully, shutting down the threat from Assyria, because Hezekiah led the people well (vv. 30-38). All in all, the king shows how godly leaders respond to crisis wisely: with reflection and humility, in partnership with prophets and the Lord, and by placing God's aims for the world ahead of all other things.

Exercise: *Which of Hezekiah's six tactics would be most helpful for you as you prepare to lead today? Meditate until you have clarity about the answer to this, and then make yourself mindful of practicing it when you are facing a decision today.*

ISAIAH 38–39

SQUANDERING A GIFT

(Isaiah said) "Some of your own sons who are born to you shall be taken away; they shall be eunuchs in the palace of the king of Babylon." Then Hezekiah said to Isaiah, "The word of the Lord that you have spoken is good." For he thought, "There will be peace and security in my days."
– Isaiah 39:7-8

King Hezekiah is a man who played a great game until blowing the lead in the last minute. He does so by trusting a military ally (envoys of Babylon) rather than turning to prayer and consulting the wisdom of prophet Isaiah. The seductive promise of Babylonian force will soon turn on Hezekiah's people and send them into catastrophic exile for generations.

What is all the more galling is that Hezekiah had just been given a new lease on life. In 38:1, he became sick and *"at the point of death."* Even the prophet Isaiah told him, *"Set your house in order, for you shall die; you shall not recover."* Yet Hezekiah wept and implored God for healing – and God did so! God said, *"I have heard your prayer, I have seen your tears; I will add fifteen years to your life"* (v. 5). God also said that in this "second term," he would deliver his people from the Assyrians.

So Hezekiah has a new lease on life and a God-given term for new leadership. But he squanders it by trusting force rather than trusting the same God who has given him and his people this new lease on life. And when Isaiah spells out the consequences – that his own sons would become captive *"eunuchs"* – instead of being mortified, Hezekiah breathed a sigh of relief at the thoughts of *"peace and security in my days."*

What kind of leader trades in the future of his or her own children for *"peace and security in my days?"*

It is a stark lesson for leaders: we to whom God has granted gifts for a chapter of leadership will be held responsible for not trading in the future of a people for our own comfort and security. Woe to the leader who sells out someone else's future. Woe to the leader who squanders a God-given opportunity to lead for the benefit of their children.

Exercise: *Is there any place where I am selling out true leadership for the false promise of security?*

ISAIAH 40

HOW LEADERS CAN HELP

*"...those who wait for the Lord shall renew their strength,
they shall mount up with wings as eagles, they shall run and
not be weary, they shall walk and not faint."*
– Isaiah 40:31

Preacher John Claypool, in his book, *Tracks of a Fellow Struggler: Living and Growing Through Grief*, describes this verse as the source of great help to him in the death of his young daughter to leukemia. When he looked for "*comfort*" (v.1) and relief from his weariness (vv. 28-30), he found that Isaiah 40:31 named three forms of "*strength*" or help that he could expect from God while waiting:

> ⊱ Miracle – "*they shall mount up with wings as eagles*" ... God intervening supernaturally to do something (make human beings **fly**!) to save;

> ⊱ Collaboration – "*they shall run and not be weary*" ... God cooperating with our effort so that we **run** (our part) but don't get tired (God's part);

> ⊱ Endurance – "*they shall walk and not faint*" ... God giving us the strength not to collapse, but to take one more step, live one more day. There is no flying or running here, only **walking**.

God sometimes intervenes miraculously, yes. But Claypool said that when he came to look for the help of God coming in **any** of these three forms, rather than expecting God to answer his desperate prayers only by miracle, he was given comfort and strength.

A leader who promises only miracles is overpromising. Not even God promises to intervene in this way alone. Sometimes we promise that form of hope. But we are also wise when we follow the way of a God who sometimes promises his help by collaboration and endurance. Leaders more often will tell those who follow that we will work hard *together* and that sometimes simply *endure* difficulty and crisis together. Miracles, collaboration, endurance – flying, running, walking - these are ways in which we can receive help and hope.

Exercise: *Which form of God's help do you most need right now? Ask for it!*

ISAIAH 41

THE RIGHT HELP

"Do not fear, you worm Jacob, you insect Israel! I will help you, says the Lord; your Redeemer is the Holy One of Israel."
– Isaiah 41:14

Praying the Prophets

The people who have the hardest time understanding hardship, suffering, and evil are those who believe in a myth of inevitable progress. Anyone who believes that things are necessarily and automatically moving toward improvement will struggle to explain failure and pain. If I am basically good and newer is better, life should move up and to the right ... shouldn't it?

But life doesn't. The worldview of the Bible is that we are sinners and we need help. Creation has been corrupted and many in this world intend harm. The strong sometimes crush the weak and the unjust oppress the just. Furthermore, Israel is a mere *"insect"* or *"worm,"* unable to solve her own problems. We need help!

Isaiah 41 says that not only do we need help, but we need the right help. In fact, calling on the wrong *"gods"* (v. 23) does more harm than good. The prophet implores these gods, *"do good, or do harm"* – that is, do **anything**. But false gods don't change life. They are merely Marx's "opiate of the masses."

On the other hand, the prophet says again and again, *"Do not fear"* (vv. 10, 13f) – because the right help is on the way. The right help is *"the Lord, your Redeemer and the Holy One of Israel."* It is a very specific God, a quite particular source of help that can dispel fear.

The function of a prophetic leader is not to act as if there is no reason to be afraid. Progress is not inevitable and there are real enemies to all that is good. Rather, leaders state plainly that we need help – or better yet, we need the right help. The good news is, for those who trust the God of the Bible, we can say with Psalm 121:1, *"I lift up my eyes to the hills – from where will my help come? My help comes from the Lord, who made heaven and earth."*

ISAIAH 42

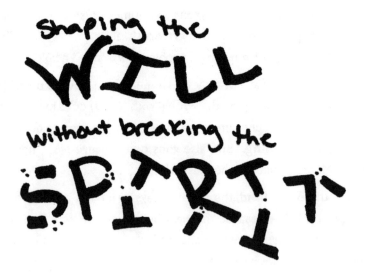

"...a bruised reed he will not break, and a dimly burning wick he will not quench; he will faithfully bring forth justice. He will not grow faint or be crushed until he has established justice in the earth; and the coastlands wait for his teaching."
— Isaiah 42:3-4

Much ink has been spilled over the identity of the servant in Isaiah's "servant songs" (in chapters 42, 49, 50, and 52). Is it Cyrus, deliverer from Persia? The nation Israel? The Lord Jesus (Matthew 12:18-21)? The whole people of God (Acts 13:47)? Yes to all of the above!

More important, though, is the nature of God's servant who leads people to "*justice*" (v. 1) and restoration (v. 22). The servant-leader is both bridge and light, mediator and missionary, warrior and woman in labor. The servant faithfully and tirelessly works to bring forth justice – "*he will not grow faint*" (v. 3), yet does so with gentleness – "*a bruised reed he will not break, and a dimly burning wick he will not quench*" (v. 3). The paradoxical combination of fierce persistence and tender carefulness is striking.

When my sons were young, I heard James Dobson's advice that the art of parenting was to "shape the will (of a child) without breaking the spirit." He said that the will of children is like iron, and the work of parents is to forge it! But the spirit of children is like a candle wick, and thus the work of parents was simultaneously to exercise great care so as not to extinguish it.

This is the way of God with us, good parents with children, and it is to be the way of leaders with those they lead. Leaders forge ahead tirelessly, fiercely, and persistently toward the mission we are given. Yet we do so without crushing the spirit of those we lead, treating people tenderly. This is the heart of servant leadership.

Exercise: *Meditate on whether those you lead today need from you the ironwork of forging or the tender care of not extinguishing.*

ISAIAH 43

"Do not remember the former things, or consider the things of old. I am about to do a new thing; now it springs forth, do you not perceive it? I will make a way in the wilderness and rivers in the desert." – Isaiah 43:18-19

Praying the Prophets

Isaiah again pronounces God's vision of hope to a beaten down people. Is there life beyond Exile? Is there a promised land where things can be different? "Yes!" says the Lord through the prophet. Chapter 43 describes both what the people need to do in order to live into that new life of hope, and what God will provide that helps people move that way.

What is required of those who hope to move toward restoration? Two things:

1. *"Do not fear"* (vv. 1,5). Anxiety is not your friend. Theologically, it is idolatry – for as God says, *"I work and who can hinder it?"* (v. 13). Anxious fear is disbelief that God is stronger than gods.

2. *"Do not remember the former things or consider the things of old"* (v. 18). More specifically, this is instruction about selective memory. Beaten-down people tend to center their identity on their hard circumstances (*"former things"*). Isaiah wants us instead to remember that we belong to a bigger, better story. Indeed, God says of us, *"you are precious in my sight, and honored, and I love you"* (v. 4).

And what does God provide for those who refuse to be defined by an anxious past?

- ⋙ *"a way in the wilderness"* – a path, highway, road, clearly marked, safe and passable on which travelers can move; and

≈ "*rivers in the desert*" – sustenance and resource for travelers on the path. Just as God provided Israel with water from a rock as she moved from Exodus to Promised Land (Exodus 17), so God will now sustain us in dry places with enough to keep us from dying of thirst.

God, our Leader, offers a way plus water, a clear path to redemption plus sustenance, vision plus food, direction plus resource. And every human leader who would ask people to forget anxious exile and move toward a new and fearless story must help them by announcing the same.

Exercise: *What "former things" in your life do you need to put aside? What event or mistake in your past is no longer worthy of your replaying and rumination? Ask God to remove the temptation to dwell on this, and, in its place, to give you the mind to think about his clear path and sustenance.*

Praying the Prophets

ISAIAH 44

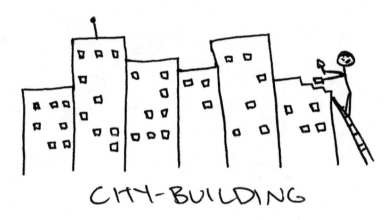

CITY-BUILDING

"(The Lord) says of Jerusalem, "It shall be inhabited," and of the cities of Judah, "They shall be rebuilt, and I will raise up their ruins …" – Isaiah 44:26

Isaiah 44 announces the hope for the rebuilding of decimated cities. Rebuilding will not happen at the hands of gods (idols) assembled or crafted by human hands (vv. 9-20). Rather, cities will be rebuilt through the agency of the Lord and his leaders. In chapter 44, one such leader is king Cyrus of Persia, of whom God says, *"He is my shepherd, and he shall carry out all my purpose"* (v. 28). God uses anointed leaders to rebuild cities.

Sociologist Richard Florida widely speaks of the rapid urbanization of the globe. For the first time in human history, more than half of the earth's population lives in cities. Why are cities so desirable? They are places where the <u>bonds</u> of close ties are supplemented by <u>bridges</u> of connection to broader social ties to people of other cultures, backgrounds, and perspectives. As such, cities are more likely to be places where creativity, innovation, and beauty flourish.

American individualism has often caused us to believe that salvation is primarily for individual souls. Good evangelical leaders call people to "let Jesus come into their hearts as personal savior." We sing, *"I come to the garden alone ...."* But the Bible begins in a Genesis 1 garden and ends in a Revelation 22 holy city. God's desire for creation is a new Jerusalem, a redeemed city. And God's anointed always work toward the rebuilding of communities, cities of beauty, truth, and goodness.

ISAIAH 45

"Shower, O heavens, from above; and let the skies rain down righteousness; let the earth open, that salvation may spring up, and let it cause righteousness to sprout up also; I the Lord have created it." – **Isaiah 45:8**

In the ancient near East, what descends from *"above"* was typically described in masculine terms, and what rises from below, in feminine. In many of these cultures, such imagery led to fertility cults – visions of the union between Father God and Mother Earth, re-enacted in the blooming of spring, harvest, etc. But while the God of the Bible retains the "above/below" frame, it paints a very different picture of how God works with his people.

For Isaiah 45, there is one God, and he alone is the initiator of creation and history. This one God operates via his *"anointed"* or *"messiah"* – here, king Cyrus of Persia, later and ultimately Jesus of Nazareth – to enact divine deliverance and salvation on the earth. In this light, the message of Isaiah 45 is that:

1. The God of heaven *"showers from above"* and *"rains down righteousness"* in initiating deliverance (Hebrew *"tsedaq,"* found 25 times in Isaiah);

2. The role of those of us on earth is to *"open"* receptively and receive God's initiative, rather than rebelling against it (Hebrew *"tsedaqah,"* 22 times);

3. The outcome of receiving God's initiative will be that *"salvation may spring up"* and *"righteousness (will) sprout up also"* – this is the creation of the Lord.

Some theologians call this "operative" and "cooperative" grace. God initiates operatively from above, and we below respond cooperatively – though even our ability to respond or cooperate is a God-given act of grace. It is through such partnership that ultimately *"every knee shall bow, every tongue shall swear"* (v. 23, later quoted by Paul in Romans 14:11 and Philippians 2:11) and *"In the Lord all the offspring of Israel shall triumph and glory"* (v. 25).

It is no accident that the best leaders are, fundamentally, <u>humble</u> and <u>cooperative</u>. They understand that their work is not that of invention and initiative, but is a cooperative response to the operative grace of God.

John P. Chandler

ISAIAH 46

THE PROMISE OF LONGEVITY

"(Listen to me ... all) who have been borne by me from your birth, carried from the womb; even to your old age I am he, even when you turn gray I will carry you. I have made and I will bear; I will carry and I will save." – Isaiah 46:3-4

Isaiah 46 is a savage mockery of would-be "savior" gods (v.1, *Bel* = "baal" or false god, *Nebo* = "savior," ironically) who used to be lauded in parades. Now they themselves must be hauled off on donkeys by their worshipers (vv. 1-2) – some saviors they turned out to be! It is a serious question of one who worships a god other than God: "How's that working out for you lately? Does your god carry you or do you have to carry it?"

Quite the opposite from gods who have been *borne* off is the God of Israel who has been with us since we were *born*. This God has created us at birth rather than having to be created by our hands. This God *carries* us, and not the reverse. Moreover, this God will be our God (the *"I AM"*) *"even to our old age."* This God promises to followers, *"Even when you turn gray, I will carry you."* He was with us in the beginning and will be with us till the end – including The End of all things.

While only God can offer an iron-clad assured future of presence, this promise illustrates something valuable for leaders. Any leader who with integrity assures followers that s/he will stay with them until the end is offering a powerful gift. Often people are willing to work through a difficult and unfinished present if they are confident that the one who leads them will stick with them until they come out on the other side. If leaders promise not to bail in the midst of unfinished business, others will give grace and get to work on the problems at hand.

We are not God and are ourselves not promised another day. And we should not over-promise. But when we can say to others, "By the grace of God, I intend to be with you until the end," this promise of longevity can be transformational.

Exercise: *Today, offer whatever promises you can make in good faith about remaining and persevering with someone you lead. Don't over-promise; but don't under-promise, either.*

John P. Chandler   93

ISAIAH 47

"Your wisdom and your knowledge led you astray, and you said in your heart, "I am, and there is no one besides me." But evil shall come upon you, which you cannot charm away; disaster shall fall upon you, which you will not be able to ward off; and ruin shall come upon you suddenly, of which you know nothing." – Isaiah 47:10-11

Isaiah 47 is a "triumph song," told from the perspective of Israel after her captor, Babylon, had fallen. It is a retrospective warning of why a dominant nation fell – why a one-time queen city now looks like a tattered servant-girl (v. 2).

Isaiah's core explanation of why Babylon fell is that she felt falsely *"secure"* (v. 10). She had too much confidence in her own *"knowledge and wisdom, enchantments, sorceries, consultations, studies, star-gazing, and predictions"* (vv. 12f). Because of this, she said, *"I am, and there is no one besides me"* – claiming for herself a title that belongs only to the Holy One. Pride goes before a fall!

Babylon, famous for her astrology and astronomy, magically believed she could secure her own future through technical mastery of the sciences of the day. This reliance on mastery of scientific technique and knowledge led her to a kind of arrogance which set her up for her fall.

Every leader is tempted to over-rely on technique, mastery of a body of knowledge, and knowledge of sciences. Of course, no leader trumpets ignorance of these things. But there is something uniquely seductive about so-called "hard knowledge" which can lead us to believe that we are able secure our future through what we know. This can lead to arrogance, unwise self-reliance, and even presumption of our own divinity.

There are no prescriptions for a better way of leading in Isaiah 47. The damage is done and it's "game over" for Babylon. The fall of a once-great city stands simply as a warning for future leaders not to inhale their own *"charm, wisdom, knowledge"* (v. 11), mastery, and ability as divine.

ISAIAH 49

"Thus says the Lord: In a time of favor I have answered you, on a day of salvation I have helped you; I have kept you and given you as a covenant to the people, to establish the land, to apportion the desolate heritages ..." – Isaiah 49:8

Walter Brueggemann describes prophecy as a "redescription of the public processes of history through which the purposes of God are given." Isaiah 49 prophesies that God will work through his broken people. Human decisions, as it turns out, are penultimate; those who would destroy the people and purposes of God will be unable to stop what God wants to do in the world. God will save and restore his broken people. God's hopes for the world will not be denied!

As one of four "servant songs" (Isaiah 42, 49, 50, 53), Isaiah 49 prophesies that God will work out his purposes in the world through his servant. God will show "*favor, answer* prayers, grant *salvation,* and offer *help*" (v. 8). God the liberator will set prisoners free and feed his sheep (v. 9), protecting his people from scorch and thirst (v. 10), and lead us on a road to life (v. 11).

But God is more than our cosmic personal problem-solver. God is interested in helping us because he has a purpose for us in the world. God saves us to send us. God restores us in order to release us on the world. God comforts us to commission us. It is a classic triangle of "Up-In-Out": salvation from God (up) heals the people of God (in) so as to cause us to be a "*light to the nations*" (out), announcing salvation "*to the end of the earth*" (v. 6).

Prophetic leaders never let us forget the "out" point of the triangle. Companies do not exist merely for their own profits. Armies are more than a career path. Nations have a calling greater than their own empire-building. Churches are more than places of refuge from the troubles of life. God works in human lives in order to mobilize us out as prophets to a world which needs to be healed, delivered, and saved. Our survival is part, but not all, of God's hopes. Purpose trumps survival.

Exercise: *Think about how concerns for security and survival might diminish your willingness to risk and work toward fulfilling your mission or purpose. Ask God for the strength to push through any instinct for self-preservation so that you can answer the call to lead well.*

John P. Chandler   97

ISAIAH 50

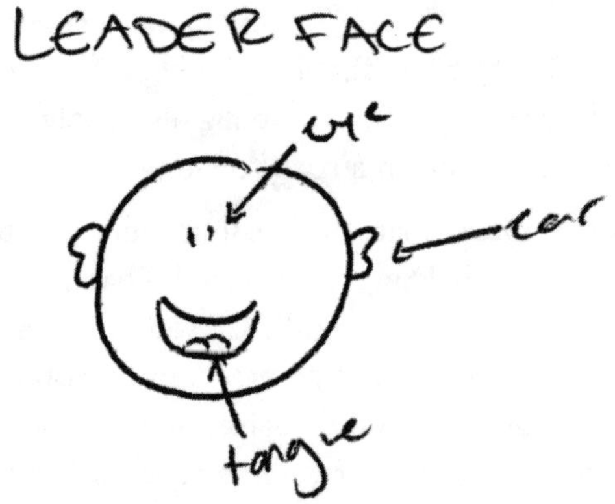

LEADER FACE

eye

ear

tongue

"The Lord God has given me the tongue of a teacher, that I
may know how to sustain the weary with a word. Morning
by morning he wakens – wakens my ear to listen as those
who are taught. The Lord God has opened my ear, and I was
not rebellious, I did not turn backward ... The Lord God helps
me; therefore I have not been disgraced; therefore I have set
my face like flint ..." – Isaiah 50:4-5, 7

These verses, spoken over me by my grandfather at my ordination to ministry, are the commission to any servant leader. Every leader will suffer, and much of it will be at the hands of insiders rather than known enemies! But I am to "*set my face like flint*" before opposition, knowing I have an advocate in the God who has called me (v. 7).

Isaiah 50's "servant song" is gathered around three images from the face:

> ॐ The blind <u>eye</u> – "*who walks in darkness and has no light*" (v. 10);

> ॐ The mute <u>tongue</u> – "*the Lord God has given me the tongue of a teacher, that I may know how to sustain the weary with a word*" (v. 4); and

> ॐ The stopped-up <u>ear</u> – "*he wakens my ear*" (v. 5 – literally "digs out" the ear in a painful form of surgery).

The prophetic leader is blind, mute, and deaf. S/he is totally dependent on God to give night vision, something helpful to say, and the ability to hear/listen. Isaiah's servant leader is not an all-seeing visionary, eloquent speaker, and sensitive listener. Rather, s/he has the face of one who "*morning by morning*" must be <u>given</u> help by God. Opposition to servant leaders will be unexpectedly strong – ask Moses, Elijah, Jeremiah, Paul, or Jesus. And it is <u>God</u> who must give servant leaders a taught tongue, open ear, and vision in the dark. That is "leader face."

The first and most important role of any flint-faced servant leader is "*morning by morning*" to receive from God the eye to see, ear to hear, and tongue to speak. In that spirit, I offer a prayer written by Thomas Aquinas that I often recite before trying to lead anyone anywhere:

> *"You make eloquent the tongues of children.*
>
> *Then instruct my speech and touch my lips with graciousness.*
>
> *Make me keen to hear, quick to learn, able to remember;*
>
> *Make me delicate to interpret and ready to speak. Amen."*

Exercise: *Which is most in need of leadership attention today: my eye, ear, or tongue?* *Whichever it is, ask God to help you put on "leader-face" today.*

ISAIAH 51

POINTING TO QUIET
EXAMPLES OF

HOPE

"Look to the rock from which you were hewn, and to the quarry from which you were dug. Look to Abraham your father and to Sarah who bore you …." – Isaiah 51:1-2

　　　　Praying the Prophets

Three times, Isaiah 51 summons people to *"listen"* (vv. 1, 4, 7). To what are they to listen and to whom are they to look? To their source and heritage, their *"rock* and *quarry,"* to Abraham and Sarah. The current exiles of Babylon are to look at how God historically worked through this original couple of exiles to *"bless"* and *"make many"* (v. 2).

Interestingly, this is the only time in the Old Testament outside of Genesis that cites Sarah. Why is she singled out here as an example toward which people should look? First, because Sarah is the opposite of the drunken whore to whom unfaithful Israel has been likened (v. 18). Instead, she is a model of faithfulness and obedience in the midst of exile. Second, God took Sarah, who was barren, and made her mother of Isaac and of many nations. Thus God can do for barren exiles what God once did for Sarah – make them fruitful again. She is a picture of redemption and hope, and to be emulated in her faithful perseverance through difficult times.

Isaiah wisely leads broken people to envision pictures of ideal response. One of the best things a leader can do to give hope is to point to examples of people who embody transformation from brokenness to salvation. And we are wise not to limit our highlighting to oft-cited leaders (like Abraham) but to point to the more quiet examples of hope, like Sarah. Find a person who is out of the spotlight but who has lived well – and often it will be a woman. Encourage downcast people to look at her life. And say, "What God has done to and through her, God can do with you."

This is the way, out of the good life of one person, that God *"blesses and makes many."*

ISAIAH 53

"Therefore I will allot him a portion with the great, and he shall divide the spoil with the strong; because he poured out himself to death and was numbered with the transgressors; yet he bore the sin of man, and made intercession for the transgressors." – Isaiah 53:12

Throughout the Bible, there are explanations of the meaning of human suffering. For instance, the purpose of suffering can be:

- ∂ Testing – as with Abraham and Isaac in Genesis 22;

- ∂ Temporary – the darkness before the surely-coming dawn (Habakkuk 2:3);

- ∂ Penal – just desserts for sinful choices (most of the book of Deuteronomy);

- ∂ Preparatory or cleansing – as with the earth after Noah's ark (Genesis 8-9);

- ∂ Mysterious – as with Job – who was rightly furious that his friends misinterpreted his suffering!

To these interpretations, Isaiah 53 adds another: suffering can be vicarious and redemptive.

No wonder that what Jews apply to the suffering of Israel has been taken by Christians to speak of Jesus and his work: "*He himself bore our sins in his body on the cross, so that, free from sins, we might live for righteousness; by his wounds you have been healed*" (1 Peter 2:24). Far from being a meaningless and unjust persecution, the suffering of the Servant is actually in service of God's greater hope to redeem people from their sins through an advocate who intercedes for their transgressions.

One of the chief works of leadership is to interpret the meaning of suffering and hardship of those whom s/he leads. As with childbirth, people can endure great pain if the pain makes sense in a larger picture. Leaders don't have to make suffering go away (as if we could!); we just have to help it make sense.

Exercise: *Using the list above, pray that God would give insight regarding the meaning or purpose of some of the suffering around you or within you.*

ISAIAH 55

WITNESS, LEADER, COMMANDER

"See, I have made him a witness to the peoples, a leader and commander for the peoples." – Isaiah 55:4

Isaiah 55 is an invitation to the great homecoming banquet of God. To all in Empire who are experiencing life as expensive, excluding, and unsatisfying, to all who "*hunger*" and "*thirst*" for more, the prophet invites them to "*buy wine and milk without money and price*" (vv. 1f). To exiles, the prophet says that God is offering a new Exodus from slavery and into a "contrast society" to which the "*nations shall run*" (v. 5). Such is the heart of the entire Bible: God invites us to a new and better feast than the table scraps this world can offer.

Isaiah's invitation is not a new one, but is grounded in what God named decisively centuries earlier in his servant, king David. David the ideal leader is described, progressively, as a). "*witness,*" b). "*leader,*" c). "*commander,*" and d). "*for the peoples.*" The order is instructive. David first bore <u>witness</u> to the initiative of God; transformation is God's idea before it is ours. Next, out of his witness to God, David was a <u>leader</u>, first to the front, beloved by his people because he was immersed with them neck-deep in solving their crises. This explains why the people (usually) gratefully allowed him to be their <u>commander</u>. He led as he did not for his own aggrandizement, but <u>on behalf of the peoples</u>, for a purpose greater than his own ego.

As David was, so Jesus would later be. And so the people of God are to be in the world today. We announce God's great party invitation as witnesses, immerse ourselves in leading others there, issue commands only out of the authority granted to us, and do all of this on behalf of a cause greater than ourselves.

God's thoughts and ways are higher than ours (vv. 8f), and only God can finally deliver his people from Exile through Exodus to the Great Banquet. But God always uses human leaders to announce and invite people to enter into this richer life.

ISAIAH 56

*"Israel's sentinels are blind, they are all without knowledge;
they are all silent dogs that cannot bark; dreaming, lying
down, loving to slumber. The dogs have a mighty appetite;
they never have enough." – Isaiah 56:10-11*

Isaiah 56-66 (called "Third Isaiah") describes life after the end of Exile. The people have been set free, restored to their homeland, and the temple rebuilt. But their hoped-for life has not yet come to pass. There is rumbling after the rebuilding. Hope is being deferred, hearts are getting sick. Loud voices are calling for the people of God to close the borders, purify the community, and "separate" from the "foreigners" (v. 3). And sadly, no leader steps up to counteract the most fearful, anxious voices in the room.

Isaiah's blunt image for *shepherds* (rulers) or *sentinels* (prophets) who neglect to counter loud reactionaries is that such leaders are bad "*dogs*." Isaiah 56 describes a bad "*dog*" or leader as:

~ "*blind*" – refusing to see God's greater vision, or the neighbors many want to exclude;

~ "*silent (and who) cannot bark*" – voiceless in warning the people about giving in to fear;

~ "*dreaming, lying down, loving to slumber*" – asleep while supposedly a *sentinel* on watch on the city wall, guarding the city from danger;

~ possessed of a "*mighty appetite* and never *(having) enough*" – self-indulgent to the point where their gluttony and drunkenness dulls them into believing they can coast, saying, "*tomorrow will be like today*" (v. 12).

Isaiah doesn't let fearful people who exclude neighbors off the hook. Woe to those who forget that God's vision is for a "*house of prayer for all peoples*" who love the Lord (v. 7). But leaders are held to a higher standard of accountability. As Spiderman says, "With great power comes great responsibility." Even better is what Jesus says: "*From everyone to whom much has been given, much will be required; and from the one to whom much has been entrusted, even more will be demanded*" (Luke 12:48).

John P. Chandler   109

ISAIAH 57

SINCERITY IS INSUFFICIENT

"I will concede your righteousness and your works, but they will not help you. When you cry out, let your collection of idols deliver you!" – Isaiah 57:12-13

Praying the Prophets

Isaiah 57 is a prophetic broadside against hyper-religious and smugly self-righteous people who worship hard, but worship the wrong gods. The prophet, in essence, warns the devout but misguided people who engage in giving offerings (v. 6), making pilgrimages (v. 9), and frequent fasting (58:3ff) that religious practices are not, in and of themselves, enough. Devotion must be offered in response to the God of the Bible – not just toward any god. The God of the Bible is one who loves the *"contrite and humble"* (v. 15), defends *"children"* (v. 5) and the weak, and delivers exiles. Other gods? Not so much.

A major league baseball star spoke of how he previously coasted on talent and made careless mistakes in the outfield. After missing a catchable ball, his manager scolded him for not catching the ball. The player responded, "I *tried* to catch it." The manager cursed him and said, "This is Major League Baseball. I can get a fan in the stands who will *try*. You are getting paid to *catch* that ball."

We are misguided when we think that "trying" or effort is enough. There is nothing magical about "devotion" per se. We are tragically wrong when we believe in the powers of "faith" and "prayer" per se. It matters to which God/god one makes devoted effort and offers faith and prayer. To be extremely devoted to the wrong god is like climbing fast up a ladder leaning against the wrong wall. Sincerity is insufficient.

Exercise: *Meditate on whether there a situation in which I am mistakenly coasting along and fooling myself into believing that my effort and sincerity are sufficient markers of my good leadership.*

ISAIAH 58

NEIGHBORLY DELIGHT

"If you refrain from trampling the sabbath and pursuing your own interests on my holy day; if you call the sabbath a delight and the holy day of the Lord honorable; if you honor it, not going your own ways, serving your own interests, or own daily affairs, then you shall take delight in the Lord, and I will make you ride upon the heights of the earth ...."
– Isaiah 58:13-14

Isaiah 58 is a broadside against worship without neighborliness. The prophet denounces Israel's piety (fasting and sabbath-keeping) when it is not matched with love toward the homeless, hungry, and naked (vv. 6f).

Three "*if/thens*" (vv. 5-9, 9-12, 13f) reinforce his core sermon: that "*delight*" is not found in "*going your own ways ... serving your own interests ... pursuing your own affairs.*" Fasting (refraining from intake) and sabbath (refraining from ceaseless productivity) are worthless as rituals if not connected with looking out for the well-being of neighbors.

Neighborliness is the path to delight. Fasting and sabbath can express neighborliness in powerful symbolic ways but are a travesty when disconnected from it. We do not find our deepest happiness in aggressive individualist autonomy. As Jesus would later crystalize Isaiah's teaching, the love of God is always expressed through the love of neighbor.

John P. Chandler   113

ISAIAH 61

"Strangers shall stand and feed your flocks, foreigners shall till your land and dress your vines; but you shall be called priests of the Lord, you shall be named ministers of our God ... " – Isaiah 61:5-6

Isaiah's oracle of hope to downtrodden Israel was a vision of hope to a beaten-down people that they would soon become like *"oaks"* (v. 3) and *"gardens"* (v. 11). Through the work of the same divine Spirit that created order out of chaos (Genesis 1:2) and deliverance from oppression (Exodus 14:21) would come radical reversal and "good news" to the *"oppressed, brokenhearted, and captive prisoners"* people of God. They will become *"priests"* and *"ministers"* (v. 6) who are saved by God to serve the world.

Jesus famously cited this vision in his inaugural sermon of Luke 4:16-30. He was also famously rejected and nearly killed for preaching it. Why? Because it is a radically inclusive vision. When the lost, least, and last are to receive prominent place and treatment in the new community of God, the special, chosen, and pure cry foul – forgetting that they too were once lost, least, and last.

Leaders rarely get in trouble for preaching purity. They often find controversy when casting vision for radical inclusivity. Like Isaiah and Jesus, prophets are to cast hopes of a community that is good news to everyone who wants a place in it.

ISAIAH 64

"Yet, O Lord, you are our Father; we are the clay, and you are our potter; we are all the work of your hand." – Isaiah 64:8

Isaiah's three mentions of God as *"Father"* are remarkable because they are, alongside of First Chronicles 29, the only such uses of father imagery about God in the entire Old Testament. Jesus would later (remarkably) call God his Father (*"Abba"*) in John 5:18 and stir great controversy by doing so.

Fatherly leadership is in this chapter connected with *"zeal, might, yearning of the heart, and compassion."* God the Father is *"potter"* to our *"clay"* – able to redeem, shape, and deliver in ways that our earthly ancestors (even Abraham and Jacob, 63:16) cannot. All of these descriptors are about proactive intervention by a passionate and capable advocate.

Noteworthy is the rare and precise biblical use of *"Father"* imagery. In patriarchal cultures there is much baggage connected with it. Most likely its best use for leaders in such cultures is not to think of themselves as fatherly, but to look to God our leader as Father, the one who does for us what no human leader is able to do. Thus we pray, *"Our Father!"*

ISAIAH 65

AGAINST FORTUNE AND DESTINY

"But you who forsake the Lord, who forget my holy
mountain, who set a table for Fortune and fill cups of mixed
wine for Destiny; I will destine you to the sword, and all of
you shall bow down to the slaughter; because, when I called,
you did not answer, when I spoke, you did not listen …."
– Isaiah 65:11-12

In response to Israel's prayer of the previous chapter, God answers with a speech of judgment (vv. 1-16) and a speech of assurance (vv. 17-25). To the latter, God promises ready availability and willingness to be engaged.

Others, however, worship gods of "*Fortune*" and "*Destiny*." (These are Syrian proper names for the gods of Luck and Fate.) Isaiah sets a scene where depending on Fortune, Destiny, Luck, or Fate is tantamount to worshiping rival gods, that is, idolatry.

John Calvin describes this as trading the vitality of conversational life with Yahweh for a settled and conventional life without risk. The promise of the God of the Bible is one of faith, not sight, of vital interaction, not a pre-set and mechanistic universe of predictability.

Biblical leaders nurture environments of relational interaction, dynamic engagement, and yet-to-be-settled work needing to be done. We are never lazily fatalistic. There is a time to recognize when the outcome of situations depends on factors outside of our control. But there is never a time to abdicate our proper role of partnering alongside of a God who wants to be engaged with us in the renewal of all things, the creation of a "*new heaven and new earth*" (v. 17).

Exercise: Ask, "*Am I, in any ways, abdicating active leadership and settling for false gods of fortune, destiny, luck or fate?*" If so, pray for God to give you a sense of your partnership today in the shared work of renewal.

ISAIAH 66

"Shall a land be born in one day? Shall a nation be delivered in one moment? Yet as soon as Zion was in labor, she delivered her children. Shall I open the womb and not deliver? says the Lord ..." – Isaiah 66:8-9

Corresponding to the rare and remarkable imagery about God as "father" in chapter 64 is Isaiah's use of divine "mothering" in chapter 66. The fatherly activity of God centers around the shaping work of God with Israel, as *"potter"* to *"clay."* Here, the primary motherly activity of God centers around *"delivery, nursing, comfort, and joy"* (vv. 7-14). Sometimes God's prime interaction with us is to change, shape, and challenge us. But sometimes, as in this chapter, God primarily interacts with us through experiences of delight, consolation, and rejoicing.

Much has been made of male and female imagery for God, and likewise much about female/male leadership. Most of it is highly political and unhelpful. A better way to frame the conversation is to think in terms of the larger biblical warp and woof of (in my friend Mike Breen's words):

- Covenant relationship and Kingdom responsibility;
- Abiding and bearing fruit (John 15);
- Identity and mission;
- Rest and work;
- Invitation and challenge.

Isaiah, like the rest of the Bible, speaks in rhythm of both the mother-like and father-like activity of God to intervene with us.

Wise leaders think likewise about their work. There is retreat alongside of advance, birth/nurture/comfort alongside of rallying the troops, joy alongside of warning, delight alongside of threat, morale as well as mission. Good mothers understand that with their children. God remembers that with us. And good leaders don't see their people simply as troops in an army but also as precious as children in whom parents would delight.

Exercise: *Spend some time now simply opening your heart to the delight that God has in you. Remember that God loves and values you first for who you are, not for what you do. Rest in the unconditional love and grace God has for you that is like a mother for a child. And as you lead today, seek to extend that same kind of love to someone else.*

JEREMIAH 1

PLUCK UP AND PULL DOWN

*"See, today I appoint you over nations and over kingdoms,
to pluck up and to pull down, to destroy and to overthrow,
to build and to plant ... But you, gird up your loins; stand up
and tell them everything that I command you. Do not break
down before them, or I will break you before them."*
– Jeremiah 1:10, 17

Jeremiah, though only a *"boy"* (v. 7; probably about age 18), was called to do the hard work of announcing God's judgment on an entitled people. Despite his youth and justified fear (vv. 8, 19), he is called to report to people who assumed they were immune because they were "chosen" that God's judgment was coming like a *"boiling pot tilted"* (v. 13).

Verse 10 captures the theme of Jeremiah's report from God. It is noteworthy that of the six verbs, four are about judgment and destruction (*"pluck up, pull down, destroy, overthrow"*) and only two about hope (*"build, plant"*). There will be dismantling before there can be reconstruction. God will clear the lot before (re)building the house. Weeding the old comes before planting the new. Christians will say that judgment precedes grace, and a cross must come before resurrection.

Jeremiah is to *"gird up (his) loins"* and dress for war. Leadership then and now is not primarily the sexy work of casting new vision and a utopic future. It typically involves the dangerous and dirty work of dethroning old and false hopes. A leader who announces a new Kingdom must first say to existing king(s), "You've gotta go!" To leaders called toward this hard work, God promises not immunity and insulation, but divine presence and finally hope: *"They will fight against you; but they shall not prevail against you, for I am with you, says the Lord, to deliver you"* (v. 19). Who will speak this hard, good word of the Lord?!

Exercise: *Is there something that needs to be dismantled, dethroned, or destroyed before God is able to utilize you for the hard work of leadership? If so, ask for God to begin to pluck it up.*

JEREMIAH 2

THE NEED FOR A COMMUNITY OF LEADERS

*"The priests did not say, "Where is the Lord? Those who
handle the law did not know me; the rulers transgressed
against me; the prophets prophesied by Baal and went after
things that did not profit. Therefore once more I accuse you,
says the Lord, and I accuse your children's children."*
– Jeremiah 2:8-9

Jeremiah 2 voices God's furious lawsuit against a fickle lover who is in denial about her disloyalty. Israel has been a stubborn ox, a wild vine, a nymphomaniac, and a thief (vv. 20-28). God speaks through the prophet as a spurned lover and stern judge. Reinhold Niebuhr once said that "Love is the willingness to take responsibility," but Israel has refused to admit her apostasy, seeking refuge in other nations instead of in her covenant with God.

At the core of this national collapse is the failure of Israel's leadership community, described in four dimensions:

> ࣿ *"priests"* – mediators of the divine presence in personal and public life;

> ࣿ *"those who handle the law"* – judges, lawyers; Israel did not answer to human kings, but, in Thomas Paine's words, "the Law is king";

> ࣿ *"rulers"* – people of power and influence in decision-making seats; and

> ࣿ *"prophets"* – those who were to speak for the voiceless.

This four-fold civic-religious partnership of checks and balances failed at every point; is it any wonder that the nation collapsed and the impact was felt for many generations to come (v. 9)?

Among many warnings, leaders can learn from Jeremiah's broadside about the importance of building a team of leaders (priests, judges, rulers, prophets), each of whom brings different perspective and role for the well-being of a whole community. Building a leadership community is not a fail-safe guarantee against trouble. But the wise leader will always look for other leaders to check, balance, and round out the ways we look to live in fidelity to our truest identity and calling. Who is missing from *your* team?

John P. Chandler 125

JEREMIAH 6

"From prophet to priest, everyone deals falsely. They have treated the wound of my people carelessly, saying, "Peace, peace," when there is no peace." – Jeremiah 6:13-14

Jeremiah thunders at his people and it is not pretty. The situation is ten times worse than Sodom. In Genesis 18, Abraham tried to find ten righteous people; here, the prophet can't even "find one person who acts justly and seeks truth" (5.1). None are found whose presence would warrant sparing the land from destruction.

Most responsible for this situation are the leaders. Of all who should not be "greedy" and "deal falsely," it should be "prophet and priest." Yet the leaders in place paper over a serious "wound" or situation with false reassurances of "Peace, peace."

Lost here are the norms by which to judge greed, falsehood, and covenantal violation. Even leaders have now lost the ability to see "where the good way lies" (v. 16) and thus how to direct people to "walk in it and find rest for your souls." These leaders believe their own propaganda and thus fail to speak the unpopular word to insensitive or even hostile audiences.

But where the truth offends our practices, leaders must speak those hard words. We cannot be so caught in the grip of a theory or ideology that we ourselves become insensitive to the consequences of sin and resultant havoc wreaked on our community (or nation). When a lightning storm is on the horizon, a leader does no favors by offering people a pacifier instead of thunder.

Exercise: *Assess whether there is some area where you are understating threat or risk (to yourself, your fellow leaders, or your followers). Resolve today to be rigorously and unblinkingly honest when it comes to speaking the truth about current or coming difficulties.*

JEREMIAH 9

A

WORTHY

(CENTER)

"Thus says the Lord: Do not let the wise boast in their wisdom, do not let the mighty boast in their might, do not let the wealthy boast in their wealth; but let they who boast boast in this, that I am the Lord; I act with steadfast love, justice, and righteousness in the earth, for in these things I delight, says the Lord." – Jeremiah 9:23

Walter Brueggemann notes that Jeremiah here presents two triads:

The two triangles represent competing religions and world views. In Jeremiah's time, as in ours, the fundamental issue is not atheism, but idolatry. The principle danger is not unbelief, but apostasy. The dominant social sin comes not from secularism but false worship. The grave danger, according to the prophet, is not a lack of transcendence. Trouble follows when transcendence is displaced from the God of the Bible and transferred to an unworthy center. Deity without transcendence destroys.

Leaders understand that people are at risk not because they don't have a worldview – they do – but trouble comes when worldview is an unworthy center for ordering our lives and the communities of which we are a part. Prophets like Jeremiah speak starkly about our "God/gods." After all, we are what we worship.

Exercise: *Ask God to reveal to you if there is any captivity in your heart to technique, might, or riches. If so, pray that you might be released today from these false gods and into a life governed by steadfast love, righteousness, and justice.*

JEREMIAH 12

"You will be in the right, O Lord, when I lay charges against you; but let me put my case to you." – Jeremiah 12:1

Jeremiah 11-20 contains six deeply personal laments from the prophet to the Lord. Jeremiah has a hard message of accountability to give to people who don't think there is a problem. The threats on his own life have already begun (11:19f). Even his own family, while smiling, is in on the treachery (v. 6) against him.

Jeremiah's response is to "take it to the Lord in prayer." He asks the unanswerable question of Job: why do the righteous suffer and wicked prosper? And even while knowing there is no answer, he asks God for permission to *put (his) case to you.*" In like manner, God's comeback to the prophet is not supportive warmth, but a further warning of tough times to come. God responds to Jeremiah with two tough proverbs (v. 5):

> ➢ *"If you have raced with foot-runners and they have wearied you, how will you compete with horses?"*

> ➢ *"And if in a safe land you fall down, how will you fare in the thickets of the Jordan?"*

God then tells the prophet that he can expect opposition from those in his family – and don't be fooled by their *"friendly words"* (v. 6). Lovely.

The bluntly honest two-way conversation between the prophetic leader and God is instructive. Jeremiah is not only talking to people but talking and listening to God. Any prophet, any leader best give only one ear to his or her constituents. The other ear and other stream of conversation belong with the leader's source of guidance, the final shaper of history.

JEREMIAH 13

"But if you will not listen, my soul will weep in secret for your pride; my eyes will weep bitterly and run down with tears, because the Lord's flock has been taken captive."
– Jeremiah 13:17

Praying the Prophets

Jeremiah 13 contains a parable (vv. 1-11), an allegory (vv. 12-14), and a simile (vv. 20-27). The images are striking: a ruined loincloth that does not enhance the appearance of the one who wears it, a drunken family, and the rape of the queen mother who is now treated like a common prisoner of war. Strong stuff.

Why the powerful and disturbing imagery? Why does the prophet use imaginative figures of speech? The answer lies in Jeremiah's despair over the stubborn unwillingness of the people to listen. "*Can the leopards change their spots?*" he asks (v. 23)? Neither can those habituated to ignore God suddenly choose to obey. God's people, as Jesus would later put it in John 8:34, have become "*slaves to sin*," unable to obey even if they were to have a change of heart and now want to obey. (In response to such situations, Jesus also often used parables and figures of speech.)

Like parents upset with the self-destructive decisions of an adult child, gone are the days of left-brain appeals to good sense. At the eleventh hour, sometimes a prophetic leader can only "*weep in secret*" at another's pride, and speak in parables, allegories, and similes in hopes of appealing to the right-brain imagination of those stubbornly bent on self-destruction.

Exercise: *If there a problem area in your life that is long-past all reasonable solutions, ask God to work in your right-brain, the seat of your imagination. Ask God to give you an image or picture which will help you to understand, cope with, endure, or address this situation.*

JEREMIAH 14-15

BEYOND
HEROES

"Then the Lord said to me: Though Moses and Samuel stood before me, yet my heart would not turn toward this people. Send them out of my sight, and let them go!"
— Jeremiah 15:1

In chapter 14, Jeremiah laments the too-far-gone condition of the people. The **threat** is total: "_sword + famine_." The **scope** is universal: "_field + city_." And the **failure** of leadership is comprehensive: "_priest + prophet_." Those who were to have led the nation in covenant obedience have instead spoken words of false reassurance and hope. To Jeremiah, though, this is nothing but a "_lying vision, worthless divination, and the deceit of their own minds_" (v. 14).

Desperately, the people cry out for a heroic leader to save the day. Just as the Israelites longed for judges like Samson and Gideon, and kings like Saul and David, so now they believe that "the right leader" could save them. But God says that even if Moses and Samuel, the two most famous intercessors in the nation's history, were to pray to God, it was too little, too late. Israel was too far gone for the talents of one leader to rescue from the mess they were in.

This is not a happy word for leaders, but it is a word for the wise. The temptation for people in trouble is to turn to a charismatic individual as a sort of savior. A nation will always be tempted to believe that if we could get the right person to intervene, all would be well. But no leader of good sense inhales that heady praise. Some problems are beyond heroes. Some ills are systemic. Some breaches are so breathtakingly wide and deep that the best a leader can do is model the way for throwing ourselves at the mercy of God and showing the rest of us how to repent or turn.

A leader always wants to believe that s/he can make a difference and is eager to get to work on that. But Jeremiah's warning to the leader is this: don't let your ego get in the way to the point of believing that you can fix anything by force of fame, charisma, or personality.

JEREMIAH 15–16

DEALING WITH ALONENESS

"If you utter what is precious, and not what is worthless, you shall serve as my mouth. It is they who will turn to you, not you who will turn to them." – Jeremiah 15:19

Praying the Prophets

In these chapters, the prophet utters his second (of six) personal laments. They are bitter complaints to God, not unlike Job's. The "*hand of God*" (15:17), so often a symbol of divine help, instead feels to Jeremiah like a crushing "*weight*" on him.

Much of what is so difficult is the powerful aloneness the prophet feels. He is not to take a wife or have children (16:1-3). He is to forsake all social relations, from those of "*mourning*" to "*feasting*" (16:5-9). Jeremiah is engaged in a powerful back-and-forth conversation with God. But as for interaction with people? Not so much.

In the face of this isolation must lay terrible temptations to relieve the loneliness. And thus God warns the prophet to hold true to his hard word in the face of any craving for company. Jeremiah is to speak what is "*precious*," not "*worthless*." No cloying words to curry favor or cultivate popularity. True community will come out of true responsiveness to God's righteous demands – indeed, "*they will turn to you*" (15:19).

We live in a culture of epidemic loneliness. Few feel it as acutely as the leader charged will telling people what they do not want to hear. Jeremiah's lament and God's warning remind leaders not to give up strong statements of truth simply to attain the companionship of people who will pat your back because you have told them they are right. True community will be found around mutual responsiveness to the true God.

JEREMIAH 18

STAYING ON THE HIGHWAY

"But my people have forgotten me, they burn offerings to a delusion; they have stumbled in their ways, in the ancient roads, and have gone into bypaths, not the highway."
– Jeremiah 18:15

Jeremiah 18 is well known for its allegory of the potter and clay. God's people, unwilling to be worked and shaped into the vessel desired by the divine potter (v. 4), will soon be discarded. The clay doesn't get to tell the potter what it wants to become!

Less well known but also powerful are the other images the prophet uses to describe the sin of faithless and stubborn people. Israel's bad behavior is unnatural, like "*mountain waters run dry*" (v. 14). Her fate is that of a victim preyed upon by a "*marauder*" (v. 22), the lion-like sin of Cain (Genesis 4:7) waiting to pounce. Pointedly, the people's folly is that of having "*gone into bypaths*" and straying from "*the highway.*" Just as sin would later be described by theologians as "missing the mark," an archery term describing a shot off-center, so Jeremiah labels the faithlessness of the people as something like getting off the main path and into a cul-de-sac.

The prophetic leader certainly must confront folly. S/he must do so with imaginative language, a flurry of images appealing not simply to human logic but to human passion. And, taking a cue from Jeremiah, the leader must call people not to be sidetracked into alleys that go nowhere. The work of the leader is to call people to stay on the good, wide, well-marked, and fast road of their central calling, in obedience to God.

JEREMIAH 20

THE RHYTHM OF PROPHETIC CONFRONTATION

"If I say, "I will not mention him, or speak any more in his name," then within me there is something like a burning fire, shut up in my bones; I am weary with holding it in, and I cannot." – Jeremiah 20:9

In Jeremiah 20:1-6, the prophet comes before the national and religious representatives of his nation, and has nothing but bad news to bring them. Like Moses before Pharaoh, Elijah before Ahab, Daniel before the lion's den and fiery furnace, and Jesus before Pilate, Jeremiah stands to speak truth to power. Dietrich Bonhoeffer would later do the same before Hitler, and Martin Luther King before a nation. Is this not the vocation of every prophet? Jeremiah is lucky only to be beaten and locked up for the treason of being so "unpatriotic" as to suggest that the nation has strayed from God and will be cursed.

How does the prophet tell a truth that is painful for everyone who hears it? The clue lies in his brutally honest prayer of verses 7-18. Jeremiah is no less honest with God than he was with people. Like Job, he lashes out against the day of his birth (vv. 14-18). Against his will, God has "*enticed*" and "*overpowered*" him with the prophetic call. His words to the nation are like a "*burning fire shut up in (his) bones*" (v. 9) that absolutely must come out.

Jeremiah endures public backlash through rigorously honest conversation with God. His are not proper and nice prayers. He is unsparing and raw both to king and King. Such is the rhythm of prophetic confrontation. Any prophetic leader finds the courage to speak truth to power by having the sort of wide-open ability to address God with the same level of intensity. The thunderous preaching of such a leader alternates between straight-up speech to people who don't want to hear it, and to a God who can bear our rawest cries.

JEREMIAH 22

ESSE
QUAM
VIDERI

"Woe to him who builds his house by unrighteousness, and his upper rooms by injustice; who makes his neighbors work for nothing, and does not give them their wages ... Are you a king because you compete in cedar?" – Jeremiah 22:13, 15

Here is Jeremiah's prophetic broadside: appearance does not make for true leadership. The Davidic kingship is not essential to the divine election of Israel. When a king becomes an oppressor, he will be removed. Despite the size and opulence of one's palace, kings have been placed by God on their thrones only for the pursuit of justice and peace for the alien, widow, and orphan. Failing that, God will remove a leader from office like a scorned lover tearing off and throwing away their "*ring*" (v. 24).

Jeremiah's harsh word is a slam against the false use of power. Kings such as Jehoiakim and Jehoiachin uncritically adopted Egyptian models of leadership, including power symbols of a "*house*" or palace built on the backs of slave labor, repeating the mistakes of king Solomon, who started off ruling in wisdom but descended into conspicuous consumption.

Cicero's "*Esse quam videri*" – "to be rather than to seem" – is the motto of my home state, North Carolina. Satirists from Machiavelli to Stephen Colbert have mockingly inverted this statement to read, *Videri Quam Esse*, scorning leaders who "seem to be rather than to be." Leaders exist to love the marginalized, the "*alien* (immigrant), *orphan,* and *widow*" (v. 3), to created communities of "*justice and righteousness.*" When they become more interested in their appearances and palaces, God discards them.

John Calvin said that the right knowledge of God comes from obedience to God. Jeremiah 22 puts it this way: the leader "*judged the cause of the poor and needy; then it was well. Is not this to know me? says the Lord*" (v. 16).

JEREMIAH 23

"See, I am against the prophets, says the Lord, who use their own tongues and say, "Says the Lord."
– Jeremiah 23:31

The land is a mess (v. 10). Public immorality runs rampant (v. 14). People are scattered and destroyed (v. 1). All the while, official religious representatives of the government tell everyone, "It shall be well with you" and "No calamity shall come upon you" (v. 17).

Jeremiah 23 explodes against court prophets who offer false assurance. Mismanaged royal and religious leadership always leads to public exile. And so-called prophets who are in bed with the royal court and thus preach "success" religion bear the brunt of Jeremiah's broadside. Don't confuse your own "dreams" with a divine "word," the prophet says (v. 28)! In your desire to "buddy up" to God, don't forget that God is transcendent, sovereign, not like us, and as free as a "whirling tempest" (v. 19)!

When learning to study the Bible, wise professors warned us against "eisegesis." Contrary to "exegesis" – to lead the intended and actual meaning out of a text of Scripture – eisegesis means to superimpose one's own bias and ideas onto the text, so that the Scripture seems to express our opinions.

Eisegesis is a temptation of every leader. We would baptize our perspective as God's mandate and cloak what we want as God's own view. The antidote is to walk with God so closely that you are terrified to tell anything else other than what you have heard God say. As Jeremiah says, "But if they (false prophets) had stood in my council, then they would have proclaimed my words to my people" (v. 22).

JEREMIAH 24

"Thus says the Lord, the God of Israel: Like these good figs, so I will regard as good the exiles from Judah, whom I have sent away from this place ... I will set my eyes upon them for good ..." – Jeremiah 24:5-6

The exile of Israel into Babylon took place in at least two stages. Those remaining behind in Jerusalem (Israel) in 597 B.C. smugly assumed that those deported (the Jews) were the objects of God's wrath. Israel also assumed they were favored by God for their own righteousness. Ten years later, they would learn the hard lesson of their pride and overly quick judgment on deported Jews.

Jeremiah 24 is a vision of good figs and bad figs, a parable of reversal. The self-righteous and self-congratulating will suffer "*disgrace, byword, taunt,* and *curse*" (v. 9). The seemingly un-favored, on the other hand, will be reckoned by God as useful: "*I will set my eyes upon them for good*" (v. 6). Turns out the bad figs aren't so bad and the good figs not so good!

Summarize it however you like:

- Don't judge a book by its cover;

- Don't be too quick to judge;

- Don't pull your shoulder out of joint patting yourself on the back;

- The arc of history bends slowly, but it bends toward justice.

For leaders reading Jeremiah's vision within the larger story of Scripture is the reminder that we are what we are by the astounding grace of God. We will be good only because God says to us "*I will give them a heart to know that I am the Lord*" (v. 7). Like Abraham (Genesis 15:6), we are "*reckoned as righteous.*" God astonishingly values those whom the world despises. God uses those not esteemed by popular opinion. God chooses those whom the "*wise*" of the world deem "*foolish*" (1 Corinthians 1:27-28).

Leaders remember this and look with love upon those forgotten by the world but remembered by the Lord.

John P. Chandler 147

JEREMIAH 25

PERSISTENT MESSAGING

"For twenty-three years ... the word of the Lord has come to me, and I have spoken persistently to you, but you have not listened. And though the Lord persistently sent to you all his servants the prophets, you have neither listened nor inclined your ears to hear when they said, "Turn now ...."
– Jeremiah 25:3-5

Jeremiah 25 is an "I-told-you-so" summary of what has gone wrong. All nations, from Egypt to Babylon, stand under the final judgment of God, and judgment always begins with God's people, Jerusalem and Judah (vv. 15-26). Contrary to popular public opinion, which is that Marduk, god of the Babylonians has won, the God of the Bible is Lord of history, even when that history includes suffering, catastrophe, defeat, and death. Later in the Bible, we will learn that the staggering divine *"cup of wrath"* which all nations will drink can be overcome by another cup – the one God's own Son would drink (Matthew 26:27).

From a leadership perspective, it is noteworthy that Jeremiah highlights his consistent, persistent, and multi-voiced messaging. For *"twenty-three years"* and through many *"servants and prophets,"* God has warned his people with the same message of repentance. Sadly, that persistent messaging has been matched with equally stubborn resistance and refusal to hear for decades; hence the divine judgment.

Leaders understand that they do not get their ideas through to people in sound bytes and by stirring half-time speeches. Moving communities takes on-point messaging over the course of many repetitions. Even then, there are no guarantees that people will follow. Nonetheless, without persistent messaging, people have no chance to follow.

So have your "elevator speech" ready. Make the same speech on every ride. And understand that it will take many rides on the elevator before communities and nations *"turn"* in new directions.

JEREMIAH 26

MORAL LEADERSHIP
IN UNEXPECTED PLACES

"Then the officials and all the people said to the priests and the prophets, "This man does not deserve the sentence of death, for he has spoken to us in the name of the Lord our God." – Jeremiah 26:16

Praying the Prophets

Chapter 26 briefly recalls Jeremiah's sermon of impending doom on the Jerusalem temple. The chapter spends much more time on the public reaction to the sermon. Not surprisingly, few hearers do the happy dance at the prophet's word of divine judgment.

Ultimately, judgment is good news. Judgment means God notices. Human behavior matters. History is not random. There will be an accounting for actions. There is still time to "*amend your ways*" (v. 13).

But Jeremiah is thought to be unpatriotic and treasonous for proclaiming that God is less-than-pleased with his chosen people and will judge his holy city and temple. Thus, they want to kill the messenger. Leading the charge for Jeremiah's lynching are the "*priests and prophets*."

The only way Jeremiah's life is spared is by appeal to biblical precedent (the case of "*Micah*," vv. 18f), and by the intervention of "*the officials and all the people*," especially a wise and calm elder named "*Ahikam*" (v. 24). Surprisingly, these people stand down the priests and prophets and prevent the unjust execution of Jeremiah. They step in and prevent the shedding of "*innocent blood*" (v. 15).

One would have expected to have religious officials speaking from the high moral ground. But sometimes moral leadership comes from unexpected places. And a wise leader listens for voices of reason and righteousness wherever they may be heard, whether they come from those in "official" places or vocations or not. You don't have to be a priest, prophet, or official to speak the truth. The wise seek out truth-tellers and life-givers regardless of their status in society.

JEREMIAH 27-28

"And the prophet Jeremiah said to the prophet Hananiah, "Listen, Hananiah, the Lord has not sent you, and you made this people trust in a lie. Therefore thus says the Lord: I am going to send you off the face of the earth. Within this year you will be dead, because you have spoken rebellion against the Lord." In the same year, in the seventh month, the prophet Hananiah died." – Jeremiah 28:15-17

Jeremiah 27-28 recounts the story of two prophets, Jeremiah and Hananiah, who had competing visions of what God was doing and how people should respond. It is not possible that both can be right. One vision is decidedly untrue, wrong, and dangerous. Remembered by a scribe, it is a lesson (and warning) about listening to the correct messenger from God.

A mini-power struggle has taken place in the camp of the occupying Babylonian army, and Hananiah wishes to capitalize on the opportunity by fomenting rebellion in Judah. Hananiah believes God won't let his people suffer long, and his cheery message is for people to rebel, because the yoke of Babylon is about to be broken (27:2, 28:2ff). Jeremiah believes the opposite. If anything, he says, it's about to get worse, and public rebellion will only exacerbate the pain. Speaking for God, he says to Hananiah, "*You have broken wooden bars only to forge iron bars in place of them!*" (28:13).

Again, only one prophet can be right. History remembers that Jeremiah's version of hard news for the people was correct. His prophecy was validated by the predicted death of his rival within the year.

This encounter is a lesson for leaders about false hope, baseless assurances, unreliable guides, positive thinking, and telling people what they want to hear. Encouraging people when they instead need is a warning is dangerous. Sometimes our job is to deliver the stern word that no one wants to receive. As writer Frederick Buechner has preached, "Sometimes the Good News is bad news before it is good news." Leaders don't shy away from voicing hard accountabilities and realities. Better an unhappy truth than a happy fiction.

John P. Chandler   153

JEREMIAH 29

BUILDING, NOT EXTRACTION

"Seek the welfare of the city where I have sent you into exile, and pray to the Lord on its behalf, for in its welfare you will find your welfare." – Jeremiah 29:7

Jeremiah now pivots to the second half of his core message that God is going to "*pluck up and pull down ... to build and to plant*" his people (1:10). He offers a pastoral word of care to God's people exiled in Babylon. Rather than romantic revolutions and escapist wishful thinking of a quick return to the old way of life, they are to embrace the Exile. By living well within Exile, they will find that there is long term hope. It won't get better in "*two years*" (28:2), as some wishfully predicted. It will take "*seventy years*" (29:10), or multiple generations. There are no quick fixes. God's people didn't get into this mess quickly and won't get out of it quickly.

The prophet's long-term solution is the imperatives of disciplined habits and re-establishment of covenant community. "*Build houses, plant gardens, take wives, have sons and daughters, multiply*" (vv. 5f) – Jeremiah urges God's people to live well within Babylon rather than hive off into enclaves. As God's people create and exemplify shalom lives within a city, God begins to "*build and to plant*" hope for the future. We become salt that seasons and light that illumines (Matthew 5:13-16).

Leaders, like Jeremiah, know that there are no microwave fixes, only crockpot solutions. Those we lead will not find their true calling by being extracted from their communities but by learning to live well and invest within them. And while leaders are unafraid to pronounce hard words of accountability, they remember that judgment is never the last word. The last word is always hope. God's purposes for us are finally good. "*For surely I know the plans I have for you, says the Lord, plans for your welfare and not for harm, to give you a future with* **hope**" (v. 11). Thanks be to God!

Exercise: *What is one practical, slow, long-term way today that I can invest in the welfare of my community, to participate in the lives of those around me, and to be an agent of shalom influence in broken places?*

JEREMIAH 30

"But as for you, have no fear, my servant Jacob, says the Lord, and do not be dismayed, O Israel ... for I am with you, says the Lord, to save you."
– Jeremiah 30:10-11

God's word to his people is always "*Do not fear.*" To Abraham before an uncertain future (Genesis 15:1); to Israel trapped between a hostile army and the Red Sea (Exodus 14:13); to shepherds "*sore afraid*" at angels announcing a Savior (Luke 2:10); God's final word to us is "*Fear not!*" We fear God because only God can dispel fear.

In what scholars call the "Book of Consolation" or "Little Book of Comfort," Jeremiah gathers up scraps of old centuries-old oracles, long-forgotten mottos, and distant memories. The prophet scoops up whatever he can in order to dispel fear in the people. God has instructed him to "*Write in a book all the words that I have spoken to you*" (v. 2). Walter Brueggemann beautifully describes what Jeremiah is doing by mobilizing these words for the fearful people:

> "On the one hand, Israel must not deny its bleak present. On the other hand, however, it must not take the present with ultimate seriousness. God's sure governance of the future stands as a powerful, palpable alternative to present despair. Even in this season of wrath, other days are coming, days of God's well-being and restoration. **The poet provides a rich set of images as a bulwark against present-tense resignation** (emphasis mine). God's sovereignty precludes a deathly fate for Israel. Israel holds to powerful promises in order not to succumb to present despair." (Jeremiah 26-52: To Build, To Plant, p. 58).

Prophetic leadership involves dispelling fear. People must be set free from needless anxiety in order to devote their proper fear to God and their full attention to working toward a future alongside of God. Like Jeremiah, leaders today can contribute to full engagement toward a hopeful future by providing "a rich set of images as a bulwark against present-tense resignation."

Gather whatever words, songs, proverbs, mottos, stories, dreams, or parables you can find. In doing so, you will learn to be a poet who pulls together the old words that cause your people to lose their present crippling fear!

Exercise: *Write your own prayer that names one of your deep fears, and in the prayer, ask the great and good God of the Bible to crush the cause of this fear. Fully imagine this. And practice the discipline of remembering it during the day.*

JEREMIAH 31

"But this is the covenant that I will make with the house of Israel after those days, says the Lord: I will put my law within them, and I will write it on their hearts; and I will be their God and they shall be my people. No longer shall they teach one another, or say to each other, "Know the Lord," for they shall all know me, from the least of them to the greatest, says the Lord; for I will forgive their iniquity, and remember their sin no more." – Jeremiah 31:33-34

Part of the "Little Book of Comfort," Jeremiah 31 is a collage of nine promises from God to his people who have been crushed by Exile. Appealing both to memory and hope, the prophet announces a day when there will be an Exodus-like homecoming, and pilgrimage will once again become possible (v. 6). Jeremiah says that it will be like the joyous reuniting of a mourning mother with her prodigal children come home (vv. 15-20).

Famously, Jeremiah expresses this as God's gift of a new covenant. It is unlike the old, bilateral treaty. God will do for his people what they have been unable to do for themselves. In the new deal, God promises not only the ability to enter into a faithful relationship with himself, but also promises to give us the heart to want this and know it. Saint Augustine taught that, by this gift of divine grace, we went from "*non posse, non pecare*" ("impossible not to sin") to "*posse non pecare*" ("possible not to sin"). Yes, we still have a role to play in the covenant relationship and must do so. But God has injected a new possibility, a new horizon for us. Of course, Christians remember this new covenant possibility given to us in Jesus Christ every time we remember his body and blood in the Lord's Supper (1 Corinthians 11:23-25).

The analogy for how leaders respond is inexact, as only God can inject grace. Still, leaders take cues from the activity of God by announcing grace onto the people we lead. Like Jeremiah, through memory and hope, we announce the injection of newness into old situations. We proclaim that it is possible, by God's grace, for people to move into a future that is not wholly determined by past. Failure does not permanently determine. God is actively moving in this world toward the healing and repair of creation, reconciling all things to himself (2 Corinthians 5:17-20). Because of that divine injection of new possibility and new covenant, we are free to choose new and hopeful ways of living. And good leaders never let us forget it.

John P. Chandler   161

JEREMIAH 32

ENACTING SIGNS OF
FUTURE HOPE

"Yet you, O Lord God, have said to me, "Buy the field for money and get witnesses" – though the city has been given into the hands of the Chaldeans. The word of the Lord came to Jeremiah: See, I am the Lord, the God of all flesh; is anything too hard for me?" – Jeremiah 32:25-27

Jeremiah 32 is the most detailed account of a business transaction in the Bible. It echoes Genesis 23, where Abraham purchased a burial plot in Canaan for his wife, Sarah. In each instance, the biblical leader enacts a sign of future hope in the midst of very real present trouble through a commercial transaction.

Jeremiah simultaneously holds conversation with the king (vv. 1ff) and the Lord (vv. 15ff). In the middle of a city-wide siege which led to the desperate and total breakdown of society and commerce, Jeremiah buys a field. It is a "performative utterance," a prophetic act, a sign of future hope. It is the prophet's way of enacting the promise of God: "*Houses and fields and vineyards shall again be bought in this land*" (v. 15). Jeremiah is modeling a way toward radical trust in the God who is stronger even than present Exile. He both asks God and quickly answers his own question: "*Is anything too hard for (you)?*" … "*Nothing is too hard for you*" (vv. 27, 18). His purchase of a plot of land in a besieged city is a sign of confidence and faith in God to give a hopeful future despite prevailing evidence of decay and destruction.

Leaders must find ways to invest in a not-yet-obvious future in deeply personal and symbolically rich ways. People don't "believe their way into behaving;" we rather "behave our way into believing." By definition, one leads by being the first one to step, by faith, into the restored life promised by God, even (and especially) when such a future seems impossible because of a heavy and dark present. Just as Jeremiah engaged in a commercial transaction involving land, we enact, in tangible, physical, incarnational, even commercial ways, the future of God toward which we want people to journey. This is leadership: to live and to teach others to "*walk by faith and not by sight*" (2 Corinthians 5:7).

John P. Chandler 163

JEREMIAH 33

BEYOND PHYSICALISM

"Call to me and I will answer you, and will tell you great and hidden things that you have not known." – Jeremiah 33:3

Theologian Karl Barth taught that the heart of biblical prayer is "petition;" prayer is, simply put, "asking." While the prophet Jeremiah was a political prisoner (v. 1), God reminds him to ask, or "*call to me.*" Chapter 33 is a collection of seven oracles of hope given to an imprisoned prophet speaking to a besieged nation. Beyond the overwhelming evidence of a ruined Jerusalem, God tells the prophet to tell the people that a day is coming when there will be both wedding songs and doxologies (v. 11).

Philosopher Dallas Willard has described "physicalism" as the prevailing cultural worldview that limits all of reality to that which can be apprehended through the five senses. Physicalists think they are "realistic." These are people who want to see numbers, evidence, facts, and the bottom line. "I'll believe it when I see it" is their motto.

But over against such physicalists comes the God who enters but is not limited by mere physical reality, whose ability to create a future is not determined by the current situation, and who, as Creator, is as reliable as "*day*" following "*night*" (v. 20) to make all things new. This God tells Jeremiah to proclaim a coming city of "*joy,*" a delight to its inhabitants and a witness to the world (v.9). It is as if God is saying, "You'll see it when you believe it."

Leaders don't merely predict futures that are nothing more than extrapolations of the present trajectory. Beyond physicalism, they envision and announce pictures of flourishing and hope that are radically and discontinuously new. And when these pictures of the new "*city*" are God-given, part of the "*hidden things that you have not known,*" then they are not mere fantasy or wishful thinking. They are part of the movement of all creation and history, and based in the power of the One who can make something out of nothing, and can make all things new.

John P. Chandler   165

JEREMIAH 34-35

"You yourselves recently repented and did what was right in my sight by proclaiming liberty to one another, and you made a covenant before me in the house that is called by my name; but then you turned around and profaned my name ..." – Jeremiah 34:15-16

Praying the Prophets

Jeremiah 34 begins a twelve-chapter section of the book devoted to events during the siege of Jerusalem. Chapters 34 and 35 are placed side by side as a case study of fidelity versus infidelity in the face of siege-adversity. The stories illustrate how and how not to react under pressure.

In chapter 34, king Zedekiah sets free the slaves in Jerusalem (vv. 8-10) – and then reneges on his promise (vv. 11ff). Whether he first did so in covenant faithfulness or out of foxhole religion is unknown; the problem is his waffling. Jeremiah equates his failure to keep his promise in protecting the poorest in their community as profaning God's name (v. 16).

On the other hand, chapter 35 describes the faithfulness under pressure of a religious order, the Rechabites. Among other vows, they reject wine-drinking as a key symbol of their refusal to be corrupted by accommodation to Canaanite culture. When brought into the temple and tempted to drink (v. 5), they hold fast to their obedience (vv. 6-11). Theirs is a sacramental refusal to cave in.

The contrast is striking and lies at the heart of what Jeremiah thunders to us. Author James Michener once said, "Sports don't develop character; they reveal it." In the same way, pressure reveals the heart of who we are. Would you like to find out what you are made of as a leader? A siege will uncover that. If we are to be faithful leaders, then reacting steadily under pressure is a "tell." When pressure-packed decisions come, biblical leaders hold fast to our "*covenant*" (our most sacred promises to God and others). We don't waffle, and we refuse convenient accommodation.

JEREMIAH 36

URGENT AND ALARMED

"Yet neither the king, nor any of his servants who heard all these words, was alarmed, nor did they tear their garments."
– Jeremiah 36:24

Praying the Prophets

Jeremiah 36 is a tale of contrasting leadership responses to crisis. Jeremiah's urgency and perseverance in reading the scroll of God's judgment before Jerusalem's leaders is set starkly against a picture of the king's nonchalant dismissal of that scroll by cutting off slices of it as he reads, and throwing those slices into a nearby brazier (v. 23).

Despite obvious danger to himself (Jeremiah has been barred from appearing, v. 5), the prophet finds a way for the words of the scroll to get their hearing before the leaders who count. *"It may be"* that the proper leadership response, even at the eleventh hour, could prevent public *"disaster"* (vv. 3, 7). With inventiveness and urgency, the prophet responds to the crisis by getting Baruch as a proxy to get the Word to the leadership circles where it needed to be heard.

The king, on the other hand, lounges before a fire. Worse still, when hearing the Word, he shreds the document and throws it into the fire, thinking that this ends the discussion. Nero fiddles while Rome burns! The scroll which was to cut his heart and cause him to cut his garments is instead cut to pieces. But the Word is not so easily dismissed. What the king doesn't realize is that his "cool" (when he should have instead responded hotly) has sealed his own dark fate (vv. 29-31). The scroll will be rewritten and expanded (v. 32). The king does not have the last word; the Word of God does.

There is a time for leaders to remain cool under fire, to keep our heads about us when those around us are in panic. But sometimes leadership means responding with proper urgency when crisis demands it. It is no time for feigning macho nonchalance or a "been-there-done-that" affect. We put aside our aura of calm and control, we leave our vacation home (v. 22), and we demonstrate viscerally our personal response as a public symbol of leadership.

JEREMIAH 37–39

LISTENING TO CHEER LEADERS

*"The king questioned him secretly in his house, and said,
"Is there any word from the Lord?" Jeremiah said, "There
is!" Then he said, "You shall be handed over to the king of
Babylon. Jeremiah also said to King Zedekiah, "What wrong
have I done to you or your servants or this people, that you
have put me in prison?" – Jeremiah 37:17-18*

Praying the Prophets

There are two pivots in the Old Testament: the <u>Exodus</u> of Israel from Egypt, and the Babylonian <u>Exile</u> of 586 B.C. Jeremiah's encounter with Zedekiah here takes place in those days just before Exile. All of the things that God's people have clung to as the sources of their identity – the Davidic king, the land, the temple – are about to disappear. Zedekiah is a symbol of the people: weak, vacillating, secretive, and unwilling to do the hard work of repentance. Destruction is not inevitable. But is going to happen when God's people are indecisive.

In this moment, the king wants a chaplain rather than a prophet. Though he knows Jeremiah has a hard truth the nation needs to hear, he prefers the cheap grace of ridiculously optimistic jingoism. And thus the king instead listens to his princes and officials (38:1ff). Not surprisingly, these lackeys want to silence the *"discouraging"* (38:4) prophet, and they throw him down a well to die. Even after a miraculous escape from the well, Zedekiah again summons Jeremiah secretly, only to disregard his advice (38:14ff). The king knows the prophet is right; he just prefers not to listen to him.

This story represents a vast failure of leadership. National catastrophe was not inevitable and could have been forestalled by decisive action. But the king listened only to the counselors who told him what he wanted to hear. His princes tried to silence any dissenting voices as unpatriotic. Even when he knew better in private (like Pilate, who wouldn't listen to his wife and instead gave Jesus over to be crucified; see Matthew 27:19), the king lacked the public will to act upon his best, though hardest, advice. As Jeremiah said, *"If I tell you, you will put me to death, will you not? And if I give you advice, you will not listen to me"* (38:15).

The best leaders don't just listen to their cheerleaders.

JEREMIAH 39–40

IMMERSION.
NOT
EXEMPTION

"As for me, I am staying at Mizpah to represent you before the Chaldeans who come to us; but as for you, gather wine and summer fruits and oil, and store them in your vessels, and live in the towns that you have taken over."
– Jeremiah 40:10

Jeremiah's predicted Exile has come, Babylon has conquered Judah, Jerusalem has fallen. The royals (who wouldn't listen to God) have been killed or deposed, and only the *"poor people who owned nothing"* (39:10) were left in the land. Into this situation enters Gedaliah to rule *"among the people who were left in the land"* (40:6).

Gedaliah rules well. He advocates neither fierce independence from Babylon nor all-subordinate accommodation. He *"represents (the remnant) before the Chaldeans* (Babylonians)*"* and is not a simple lackey. His advice is for the remnant people to get busy and rebuild the city. *"Gather ... store ... live in the towns you have taken over."* His leadership is to make a broken city work well again. He guides people to make the economy work, make the spiritual life of the community work (41:5). His moderate, pragmatic voice gains Jeremiah's approval as he finds a middle way to govern between military hawks and opportunistic quislings.

Gedaliah's one flaw is a fatal one: he fails to heed the warning of his allies about an assassination plot on his life (40:13-16), which is carried out by a thug named Ishmael (41:1-10). His early death sends the city spiraling back into chaos, undoing much of the gains of rebuilding. As a leader, he has been *"harmless as a dove"* but not *"wise as a serpent"* (Matthew 10:16). This failure was costly. A leader has to learn to trust in God's goodness without turning a blind eye to very real evil. It is a serious warning.

But for the most part, Gedaliah's leadership is exemplary. He leads by governing in places where things are broken. Leadership always means jumping into tough situations rather than getting a hall pass to sit out the broken stuff. He lives in the town he wants to see fixed, and as such points toward Jesus, who would pitch his tent right in the neighborhood (John 1:14) through the Incarnation. With Gedaliah, with Jesus, with us, leadership is always immersion into the hard situations, not exemption from them.

JEREMIAH 42-43

REQUESTING AND REJECTING GUIDANCE

"Let the Lord your God show us where to go and what we should do ... Whether it is good or bad, we will obey the voice of the Lord our God to whom we are sending you, in order that it may go well with us when we obey the voice of the Lord our God." At the end of ten days the word of the Lord came to Jeremiah." – Jeremiah 42:3, 6-7

One could argue that the book of Jeremiah is basically about "listening" and "not listening." Repeatedly, leaders and people do not listen to God, and the consequences are severe and inescapable. On the other hand, Jeremiah does listen, even to the hard words, and as such is a voice of hope amidst wreckage.

This major theme is captured well in chapters 42-43. The people are in disarray following the assassination of the king. They fear reprisals from Babylonian headquarters for the local uprising. They are desperate and leaderless, and so they turn to Jeremiah and ask the prophet to consult God for them. They request guidance. In a "foxhole religion" moment, they write a blank check to the prophet (and to God), promising to obey whatever God commands in response to their request.

Though Jeremiah certainly had a well-worn stump speech handy, he waits and prays for *"ten days."* He actually stops and listens deeply to God – even in the middle of urgent community crisis. Only then does he respond with guidance: stay and work it out; escape to Egypt is a fatal miscalculation.

But unlike Jeremiah who deeply listens, the *"commanders"* and *"people"* (42:8) choose not to listen to the guidance. They abandon ship, smear the prophet's character (43:2-3), take him hostage, and flee to Egypt. They undo the Exodus. Jeremiah ironically forecasts something like the plagues (43:11) coming upon the disobedient as a result of their failure to listen.

False leaders make a show of requesting guidance, but often reject it in favor of quick fixes or easy escapes. True leaders, on the other hand, turn to God for guidance, wait long enough to hear a new answer, and then say and do whatever the Lord tells.

John P. Chandler   175

JEREMIAH 44–45

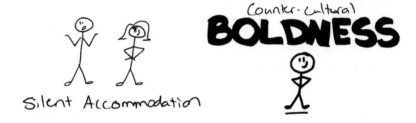

Silent Accommodation

Counter-Cultural **BOLDNESS**

"And you, do you seek great things for yourself? Do not seek them; for I am going to bring disaster upon all flesh, says the Lord; but I will give you your life as a prize of war in every place to which you may go." – Jeremiah 45:5

Praying the Prophets

These are God's final words (chapter 36-45) through Jeremiah to the people of Judah who have run to Egypt for escape, and to Jeremiah's scribe, Baruch.

Unsurprisingly, the word to the people is one of judgment: you can run, but you can't hide. God has persistently warned and *"begged"* (44:4), the people have stubbornly *"not listened"* (44:5), and no one has shown *"contrition or fear to this day"* (44:10). There is a pattern, a history. Interestingly, the people who are held to account for this are the *"men who were aware that their wives had been making offerings to other gods"* (44:15, 19). Like Adam standing dumbly by Eve as she strikes a bargain with the serpent in Genesis 3, these husbands never resisted the apostasy in their households. They never spoke up, never stepped in, never intervened in the folly. They did not lead within their own households. This benign neglect is all the more striking in a highly patriarchal culture.

The counter-witness to this lazy accommodation is Baruch. Faithfully dictating for Jeremiah, he personally pays for it (45:3). As with Job, God promises no great comforts, but only spares his life (44:5). Baruch and Ebed-melech (38:7-13, 39:15-18) become echoes of Joshua and Caleb (Joshua 2), archetypal bold leaders who brought the faithful minority report about God's work in Canaan.

So, we have one picture of lazy silence in the households, and a second picture of minority boldness. For leaders, the contrast could not be clearer. To those who might say, "You have to go along to get along," we are reminded that leadership is not measured by popularity, nor is the word of God to us gauged by how comfortable it makes people (including us). God has a persistent word to say to the world, and the prophetic leader will be faithful to give voice to the clear demands of God.

Exercise: *Is there a "minority report" to which you need to listen today? Make a point of giving your ear to an unpopular voice as a potential source of hard-to-hear and demanding truth.*

John P. Chandler

JEREMIAH 46

"Give Pharaoh, king of Egypt, the name "Braggart who missed his chance." – Jeremiah 46:17

Praying the Prophets

The book of Jeremiah ends with a collection of oracles against the enemies of God's people. Chapters 46-51 ends with an oracle against Babylon, the current reigning enemy of Israel (chapters 50-51). It begins with an oracle against Egypt, the prototypical enemy of God's people and God's purposes. Any time you hear "*Egypt*" and "*Pharaoh*" in the Bible, your mind should go back to the decisive work of God for Israel against Egypt in the Exodus. The nations are judged because Jeremiah wants his downtrodden people to remember that God is watching, final accountability is certain, the downtrodden are remembered, and all human power is subject to divine power.

In chapter 46, God judges Egypt for its autonomy and arrogance. The Pharaoh makes the fatal mistake of attributing to himself a power and ability that belongs only to God. He is a "*braggart.*" And he has "*missed his chance*" to acknowledge his subjection as a ruler to the Lord of history ... thus he will be destroyed along with his whole nation.

Leadership is not correlated with braggadocio. Just because a leader makes grand claims and acts boisterously, s/he is not exempt from God's rule over history. A leader leads at the pleasure of God, the Leader of history. We steward. God limits, curbs, chastises, punishes, and governs – and this is true of human leaders, of nations and of history.

JEREMIAH 49

"Accursed is the one who is slack in doing the work of the Lord; and accursed is the one who keeps back the sword from bloodshed. Moab has been at ease from his youth, settled like wine on its dregs ..." – Jeremiah 48:10-11

Jeremiah 49 is a collection of oracles with divine judgments against neighbors of Judah who stood idly by while the people of God were carried into exile by Babylon. These from *"Moab"* will be cursed with the same bitter fate as the exiles, not unlike those in Europe who said nothing while Hitler persecuted the Jews and invaded nearby nations.

A central and powerful image in the curse strikes at Moab's reputation for good wine. Wine is a gift from God *"to gladden the human heart"* (Psalm 104:15). But in excess, wine leads to drunkenness that is a *"mocker"* of God and neighbor (Proverbs 20:1). Moab's leaders have *"been at ease"* when they should have been vigilant and come to their neighbor's defense. Because of too much *ease*, too much metaphorical wine, Moab will also *"wallow in his vomit; he too shall become a laughingstock"* (v. 26).

Ease, like wine, or like Sabbath, is a gift from God to the world. It is a particular gift to leaders who are frequently under pressure. God gives rest to leaders as a way to recharge them for the demands of their role. But if rest and ease become ends unto themselves, they can take the leader off of his or her post. Too much ease is like wine gone sour. Woe to the leader who never rests. But woe to the leader seduced into a life of privilege and ease, and who becomes insulated from the proactive responsibilities of vigilant neighborliness.

Exercise: *Sloth or acedia is a sort of stupor that leads to lack of caring for those around you. Are there any habits that are dulling your attentiveness to others? Pray for God to reveal this to you, and if there are any, ask for God to pull back from them.*

JEREMIAH 50-51

HISTORY IS A TRIANGLE

"Remember the Lord in a distant land, and let Jerusalem come into your mind ..." – Jeremiah 51:50

The final set of Jeremiah's "oracles against the foreign nations" (chapters 46-51) are here directed against the current ruling power, Babylon. Chapters 50-51 collect at least thirteen sets of warning metaphors to the Babylonian nation currently being used as *"my war club, my weapon of battle"* (51:20) – God's hammer to *"smash"* (vv. 20-23) disobedient Judah.

The warning is this: history is not, in Henry Ford's words, "just one (*&%!) empire after another." History is not a two-way tug-of-war between existing and emerging super-powers. History is instead a triangle:

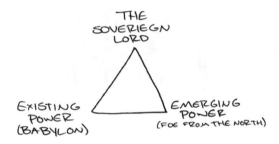

Life beyond the oppressor Babylon is imaginable for God's people, because Babylon is not finally the determiner of history. Today's hammer will be tomorrow smashed due to abuses of power. Only one *"King"* rules, and his name ain't Nebuchadnezzar! The true King's *"name is the Lord of hosts"* (51:57).

This is both a word of hope to the oppressed, and a warning to leaders in charge. Human leaders serve under the larger sovereignty of God. A leader is a tool for the divine purpose in history. The leader's best attention is not to be given to those under their thumbs, nor to those who threaten their might (an emerging power), but to the true King (The Sovereign Lord) at whose pleasure they serve. Jeremiah's message to leaders is thus for proper hope against despair, and for proper humility against arrogance. History is not a tug-of-war, but a triangle, with God the King at the top.

John P. Chandler   183

JEREMIAH 52

HOPE IN PRISON AND EXILE

"In the thirty-seventh year of the exile of King Jehoiachin of Judah, in the twelfth month, on the twenty-fifth day of the month, King Evil-merodach of Babylon, in the year he began to reign, showed favor to King Jehoiachin of Judah and brought him out of prison; he spoke kindly to him, and gave him a seat above the seats of the other kings who were with him in Babylon." – Jeremiah 52:31-32

Not for nothing is Jeremiah known as the "weeping prophet." His entire message of doom has come to pass with the destruction and desecration of Jerusalem. Exodus is undone. Samuel's ancient warning (1 Samuel 8) about "what happens when you ask for a king" has come to pass. The capital city of God's people is in shambles, with only the poorest left behind. The sitting king, Zedekiah, who has been spiritually and politically blind, is now physically blinded (v. 11), bound, and imprisoned. Chapter 52 is Jeremiah's "I told you so!"

Yet even amidst the wreckage, are signs of remnant hope. "*Artisans* and *vinedressers*" (v. 16) are left behind in Jerusalem to till the soil. And after "*thirty-seven years*" (!), Jehoiachin, king of the line of David, is restored from prison and treaded "*kindly.*" The final (true) king is not about blindness and death; the final king is about restoration and hope. Might God still do the same for his people? We know that another King, a Savior, from the line of David would one day be born (Matthew 1:1) – in over five centuries!

Jeremiah, for all of his naysaying, gloom-and-doom, and threatening, can't help but end his words with a note of hope. Every good leader has to do the same. Not a fast hope (thirty-seven years) or a false hope ... but the hope that comes from God who is more powerful than Empire, and who works through human history to carry out purposes far more powerful than the wishes of any king or sins of any people.

LAMENTATIONS 1

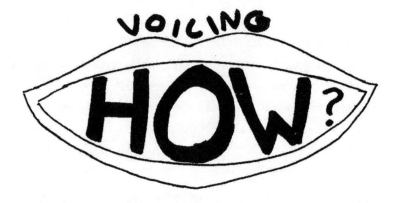

"How lonely sits the city that was once full of people! How like a widow she has become, she that was once great among the nations!" – Lamentations 1:1

The book of Lamentations is a collection of five acrostic dirges to be recited publically on days commemorating national disaster. Full of brutal imagery and frank in admitting human sin, they "lament" the broken city (Jerusalem) and desolate nation (Judah). In the face of Auschwitz-like suffering after Babylonian Exile, the lyrics give voice to the grief of a heart-broken people who stand in the rubble of atrocity. The very first word signals the question behind the whole book: "How?" How could this happen? How could you, God, let this happen? How did we get in such a mess? How do we get out of here? How can any of this make sense?

It is a book without characters, plot, and argument. Most of its hopes simply wish and flail – "See, O Lord, how distressed I am; my stomach churns" (v. 20). "Deal with them (the perpetrators of Exile) as you have dealt with me" (v. 22).

So what is the purpose of Lamentations, and what might any leader learn from it?

One way to look at it is to understand that lamentations give voice to the voiceless. They utter the unutterable. There is power, as theologian Stanley Hauerwas puts it, in "naming the silences." When we do this, we not only speak <u>to</u> people, we also speak <u>for</u> them. We say for and with our people what they would say if they could only find the words. Whether a communal liturgy, or a leader speaking before a broken people, voicing the "How?" is a powerful work of hope. It is an act of leadership that both affirms and expresses hope for a coherent world in the middle of confusing times.

LAMENTATIONS 2

"He (God) *has broken down his booth like a garden, he
has destroyed his tabernacle; the Lord has abolished in
Zion festival and Sabbath, and in his fierce indignation has
spurned king and priest ... Her gates (Jerusalem) have sunk
into the ground; he has ruined and broken her bars; her kin
and princes are among the nations; guidance is no more, and
her prophets obtain no vision from the Lord."*
– Lamentations 2:6, 9

Praying the Prophets

Lamentations 2, like the book of Job, empowers by voicing human despair, by "naming the silences." Here, it laments the complete breakdown of all forms of mediation between God and his people. Physical points of contact are in ruins – the "booth" or "tabernacle" is "broken down" (v. 6), the "altar and sanctuary" scorned (v. 7), the "walls" of the city of God "in ruins" (v. 8), "gates and bars" have "sunk into the ground" (v. 9).

Because of this destruction, "guidance is no more" (v. 9). All human forms of leadership disappear. "King and priest" are "spurned." Prophets either "obtain no vision from the Lord" or see "false and deceptive visions" and "misleading oracles" (v. 14).

Access to God is gone. The overall outcome of the decay is that God's people are no longer able to experience "festival and Sabbath." These are the prime gifts from God to his people and from his people to the world. And now they are gone.

Boundaries, structure, discipline, ritual, laws, set-apart sacred space ... all of these are necessary both to distinguish the human from the divine, and also to mediate their connection. God has never tolerated and will never tolerate human disregard for these critical boundaries. When we insist on violating them, "festival" joy and "Sabbath" rest disappear.

And so a good leader doesn't tell her or his people to live recklessly outside the box, color outside the lines, boldly go where no one has gone before. The myth of always breaking boundaries as the key path to innovation and life can actually be the way to ruin, to the complete loss of access to life, guidance, joy, and rest. Without boundaries, there are no festivals.

LAMENTATIONS 3

"The thought of my affliction and my homelessness is wormwood and gall! My soul continually thinks of it and is bowed down within me. But this I call to mind, and therefore I have hope: The steadfast love of the Lord never ceases, his mercies never come to an end; they are new every morning; great is your faithfulness. "The Lord is my portion," says my soul, "therefore I will hope in him." – Lamentations 3:19-24

Longest of the five laments, Lamentations 3 is the literary and theological center of the book. It is an acrostic poem in three parts, the middle of which voices a wise sufferer calling on past memories of God's help and hope. Under great duress, the center of the book recalls the Lord's old promise to priests (Numbers 18:20) to be their *"portion."* During distress, why is this ancient memory so centrally featured?

Poet Czeslaw Milosz (*The Witness of Poetry*, p. 68) notes that during World War II trauma, Polish victims of German occupation expressed their state through thoroughly conventional memories and metaphors. "Small devices" already in the repertory, traditional motifs available even in the most upsetting times – these were the vehicles through which victims dealt with primal suffering. This is what happens in Lamentations 3 – when every bit of topsoil has been scraped away through pain, old memories of God's promises and deliverance bubble to the surface from the depths.

Thus we sing hymns like *"Great is Thy Faithfulness"* at weddings and funerals. It is why Christians have traditionally cited the twenty-third Psalm, the Lord's Prayer, and the "Jesus Prayer" (*"Lord Jesus Christ, son of God, Savior, have mercy on me, a sinner,"* or the short form, *"Lord Jesus, have mercy"*) in times of extremes.

While slogans, mottos, and metaphors can be terribly misused, the wise leader will seek to put a stock of key metaphors of hope into the banks of memory of those s/he leads. If people have these go-to "small devices" hidden in their hearts, they will be a great source of comfort, help, and hope against the toughest times. In that painful day, they will help us say the unsayable.

Exercise: *Remember repeatedly a verse, prayer, motto or proverb that will be useful for you today.*

EZEKIEL 3

INTERNALIZE

"He said to me: Mortal, all my words that I shall speak to you receive in your heart and hear with your ears; then go to the exiles, to your people, and speak to them. Say to them, "Thus says the Lord God"; whether they hear or refuse to hear ... The spirit lifted me up and bore me away; I went in bitterness in the heat of my spirit, the hand of the Lord being strong upon me. I came to the exiles at Tel-Abib, who lived by the river Chebar. And I sat there among them, stunned for seven days." – Ezekiel 3:10-11, 14-15

The prophet Ezekiel is a street preacher given a tough ethical message to speak to stubborn people dislocated from all they have ever known. His visions are described in wildly symbolic language because their exile problems and solutions do not lie in merely the pragmatic world, but in the transcendent realm. His audience is full of questions about access to God – "Where is the Lord?" But few will do the happy dance once Ezekiel reminds them of their personal responsibility for their present and future state. It is a hard (though necessary) "tough love" message to be given to an unreceptive people.

Ezekiel's "call story" is the second longest in the Bible (behind only Moses). In it are patterns for how God calls every leader who will be given a tough assignment. First, Ezekiel is to *"eat this scroll"* (v. 1). His message isn't his own but is given to him by God. His first work is to digest what is given.

Second, he is to go to his people and to be fully present before speaking. Remarkably, in this time of crisis, instead of quick action, the prophet *"sat there among them, stunned, for seven days"* (v. 15). God tells him to *"Go, shut yourself inside your house"* and not speak. Only after the prophet is properly present among his people will God then give him the tough message to say to them – a message of personal judgment, ethical responsibility and ultimately of divine presence and hope.

The late Steven Covey famously taught the habit of, "Seek first to understand, and only then to be understood." Ezekiel's call models the same thing. Leaders don't come into a dire situation with a pre-made speech, guns-a-blazing. They listen for God's message, digest it, and sit with the people to whom they will give a hard word. They first internalize and are present. Only then do they have the right to say to anyone, *"Thus says the Lord."*

EZEKIEL 4–5

THE POWER OF A MIME

"Then lie on your left side, and place the punishment of the house of Israel upon it; you shall bear their punishment for the number of days that you lie there." – **Ezekiel 4:4**

The prophet Ezekiel begins his street-preaching ministry with silence and presence. Though he receives powerful revelation from God about what is and what is to come (chapter 1), he is then instructed to digest what he has heard from God (*"eat what is offered to you; eat this scroll"* – 3:1) before speaking. He sits among his Exile audience for a long time without ever speaking (3:15, 24ff).

Chapters 4-5 are Ezekiel's first public message. Yet, instead of a verbal sermon, he performs a mime in three acts. He stages a siege scene using a brick and iron plate (4:1-3). Then he lies on one side and then the other for a set number of days while eating only starvation rations (4:4-17). Finally he shaves all over and destroys the hair in thirds by burning, cutting, and scattering, saving only a remnant (5:1-17). These are strange object lessons, but they are not cryptic. His one-man theatre communicates his message publicly and quite clearly.

Communicators have long understood that what communicates most are non-verbal cues. Leaders would be wise to understand the power of a symbolic action that mimics and encapsulates later verbal messages that follow. When an audience has long ago forgotten the words of our speeches, they will well remember a powerful demonstration of a symbol or mime that represents the heart of what we wanted to say.

After all, while few today can quote the Sermon on the Mount at length, many can understand the meaning of Jesus' life and death when they see a cross.

Exercise: *What message are you trying to communicate to those whom you lead? What would be a physical symbol or a short mime that captures the heart of that message? Spend some time in prayerful imagination of that – and of how best to use it on your public platform of influence.*

John P. Chandler

EZEKIEL 6-7

CRUSHING FALSE HOPE

"Thus says the Lord God ... I, I myself will bring a sword upon you, and I will destroy your high places. Your altars shall become desolate, and your incense stands shall be broken; and I will throw down your slain in front of your idols."
– Ezekiel 6:3-4

Ezekiel begins his ministry in silent presence among the Exiles to whom he preaches (chapters 1-3). When in chapters 4-5 he takes the pulpit, so to speak, he first performs mimes to demonstrate symbolically what he is about to say. Not until chapters 6-7 do the verbal sermons begin – and boy, are they doozies.

The prophet's opening salvos are bluntly graphic to the point of being scatological: your *"idols"* (literally, dung-balls!) are about to be destroyed, you will lose control of your bladders (7:17 – *"all knees will turn to water"*), and nothing in which you have trusted can save you. Not commerce (7:12f), not armies (v. 14), not *"silver and gold"* (v. 19), not your Temple (vv. 20f), and no leader or *"king"* … nothing can save you from the disaster that is coming.

Why the harsh opening salvo? Because Ezekiel's nation underestimated the seriousness of her (self-induced) problems. They casually trusted in their historic and exclusive relationship with God to spare them from anything beyond temporary and inconvenient trouble. No, says the prophet, The Day is coming, and it will prick your superficial hope like a balloon.

Pioneering leaders can be prone to a default approach to problems that tends toward solving them with positivity and optimism, energy and enthusiasm. Work hard, keep people excited, pump them up, tell them that they are going to win! But we learn from Ezekiel that, sometimes, the leader is called to tell the people that it's bad – really bad. And that it's going to get worse. When people are complacently and falsely hopeful, a leader is called to tell them unpleasant truths about themselves and their future, words that pull a scab as a first step toward draining an infection.

Painful, unpleasant, and graphic, yes. Necessary? You bet. For we who follow Jesus Christ know that his cross preceded his resurrection. And crushing false hope is the first step to discovering true hope.

John P. Chandler

EZEKIEL 8-11

"Then he said to me, "Mortal, have you seen what the elders of the house of Israel are doing in the dark, each in his room of images? For they say, 'The Lord does not see us, the Lord has forsaken the land.'" – Ezekiel 8:12

Ezekiel 8-11 is the longest ecstatic vision in the book. It is a confusing account that includes a sort of "soul travel" unparalleled in the Bible. At the heart of its many scenes, though, is a core message: Israel is in big trouble because she has corrupted her unique devotion to Yahweh. Call it compromise, syncretism, interfaith mash-up – from the vantage point of Ezekiel the priest/ prophet, God's people have broken the first two commandments: to love God supremely, and to neither make nor bow down to idols (Exodus 20:2-6). (Interestingly, the prophet notes that this leads to *"filling the land with violence"* (8:17). If you pollute the command to love God, you will see the breakdown in human relationships.)

The *"elders of the house of Israel"* have misled the people by incorporating elements of the worship of other national gods into the temple of the Lord. Whether Egyptian (8:7-13) or nature religion (8:14f, 16-18), the incense of this compromised worship is a stench in the nostrils of God (8:17). Inspection (chapter 8) will lead to verdict (chapter 9) will lead to judgment (chapters 10-11). Apostasy combined with self-righteous overconfidence (11:15) is a deadly combination!

Why does this scripture so decisively condemn what could look like noteworthy tolerance and respect of neighbor's differing beliefs? Because we neither honor our neighbors nor our God when we hand over our own core identity bit-by-bit. The God of the Bible demands exclusive loyalty. The failure of religious leaders in Ezekiel is that they gave away the farm.

Leaders understand and acknowledge the place of differing world views around them. But they do no favors when they sell out their unique identity through offering a people-pleasing mishmash of world views, where everyone has their say, and everyone's say is equally valid. To do so is not enlightened tolerance and necessary compromise. It is weak-willed pollution and syncretistic apostasy. It demonstrates a lack of confidence in God to save, and it is a failure of leadership.

John P. Chandler 199

EZEKIEL 12

"The word of the Lord came to me: Mortal, eat your bread with quaking, and drink your water with trembling and with fearfulness; and say to the people of the land, Thus says the Lord God concerning the inhabitants of Jerusalem in the land of Israel: They shall eat their bread with fearfulness, and drink their water in dismay, because their land shall be stripped of all it contains, on account of the violence of all those who live in it." – **Ezekiel 13:17-19**

One or two years into his preaching, people were still shrugging off Ezekiel and his message. *"He prophesies for distant times"* (v. 27), they say. As in chapters 4-5, Ezekiel persists by enacting two living parables (digging through his house in v. 5, and eating siege rations with trembling in v. 17). He tries to become a living *"sign"* (v. 11) for his yawning people, in hopes that *"Perhaps they will understand, though they are a rebellious house"* (v. 3). Complacency and apathy can be more deadly than outright hostility!

At this point, it is fair to summarize Ezekiel's actions as marks of a true prophet. (We will see marks of a false prophet in the next chapter.) A true prophet:

1. Lives in the midst of the people to whom s/he is prophesying (12:2).

2. Demonstrates the message with actions as well as words (12:3ff, 18).

3. Follows God's revelation with exacting detail and precision.

4. Is willing to risk humiliation and unpopularity for the sake of telling the true message (12:9).

5. Interprets the message so the people can understand (12:10).

6. Removes false sense of security derived from conventional wisdom (12:23).

7. Speaks with great urgency (12:28).

These are guideposts as to how can we discern whether a leader and his or her message is from God. Does the leader live humbly and have spiritual integrity? Does s/he enact the message? Is s/he persistent with the rebellious? Does the message primarily involve and advance servanthood? Does the leader tremble at the fate of those ignore what is truly fearsome? These are marks of a true prophetic leader.

EZEKIEL 13

"Thus says the Lord god, Alas for the senseless prophets who follow their own spirit, and have seen nothing! ... You have not gone up into the breaches, or repaired a wall of the house of Israel, so that it might stand in battle on the day of the Lord." – **Ezekiel 13:3, 5**

Having described marks of a true prophet in chapter 12, Ezekiel wheels around and lambasts those who have abdicated spiritual leadership in time of crisis. His harshest words are for those in a position to enter the difficulties of the day, but who refuse to engage, and thus leave Israel unfit for the difficulties of coming days. If a true prophet comes with tough love, a false prophet is socially irresponsible and tells people what they want to hear instead of what they need to hear. As Jesus would later say "*Woe!*" to false leaders of his day (Matthew 23), Ezekiel's core metaphor of false prophets is that they "*whitewash*" rather than repair the city's walls (vv. 10-16). To summarize,

A False Prophet:

1. Creates the message out of his/her own imagination but passes it off as divine (vv. 2f, 7).

2. Misleads people into a false sense of security (vv. 10-16).

3. Fails to prepare people spiritually for tough times (vv. 10-15).

4. Is pre-committed to the status quo and is thus unable to challenge injustice (v. 19).

5. Looks and sounds like an authentic prophet, but absorbs pagan practices (vv. 17-22).

6. Leans on "magical" solutions to real problems (vv. 17-19).

7. Preys on vulnerable people for personal gain (vv. 18-21).

Leaders in Ezekiel's day and ours listen for those who can advise us into an uncertain future. When we hear counsel marked by any of these signs, watch out! And woe to us if we ever misuse our places of leadership in false ways.

John P. Chandler   203

EZEKIEL 14–15

ESTRANGED BY ATTACHMENTS

"Mortal, these (elders) have taken their idols into their hearts, and placed their iniquity as a stumbling block before them; shall I let myself be consulted by them? ...all of whom are estranged from me through their idols." – Ezekiel 14:3, 5

The ancient arrangement – that God would reveal his hopes for the world through the shining example of Israel – is now dead. It is *"charred"* wood, *"consumed by fire"* (15:4), useless. At this point, false hopes that a hero can step in and save the day are useless against this verdict of judgment. The old hopes for the nation are so far gone, says Ezekiel, that even the intercession of the famously righteous *"Noah, Daniel, and Job"* (14:14, 20) wouldn't alter the situation.

The breakdown occurred because of idolatry: the *"hearts of the house of Israel … are estranged from me through their idols"* (14:5). These idols are a *"stumbling block"* (14:3) to open communication with God. Idols are competing attachments that interfere with the core divine-human relationship. Even if Israel wanted to hear from and speak with God, she could not; her pre-commitments to idols drowned out any signal.

A leader understands that people are sometimes unable to respond positively to new vision because they are already committed to other visions. Thus in Dallas Willard's words, people first must be taught to "abstain" from some old things before they can "engage" with some new ones. You have to clear the lot before you build the house. You erase the board before writing something new on it. A leader must first purge people of competing existing attachments before prompting new ones. Otherwise, s/he is simply papering over many layers with one more layer.

And if people are unwilling to *"repent and turn away"* (14:6) from their existing (and competing) attachments, then not even a hero can lead them into a new day and place.

Exercise: *Is there an "attachment" that is standing in between your heart and the ability to communicate openly with God or another person? What needs to be removed or cleared in order to build that relationship?*

EZEKIEL 16

SHOCKING PEOPLE
OUT OF ENTITLEMENT

"This is the guilt of your sister Sodom: she and her daughters had pride, excess of food, and prosperous ease, but did not aid the poor and needy. They were haughty, and did abominable things before me; therefore I removed them when I saw it." – Ezekiel 16:49-50

While preaching a series of allegories (Israel's situation is a vine, an eagle, a cedar branch), Ezekiel 16 is an allegory so scandalous that it has embarrassed preachers to this day. Jerusalem is like an unwanted baby who survives to become a maiden. The young girl is rescued and wooed by God to be a bride. But the bride soon repays this grace with unprecedented and ungrateful promiscuity. The prophet tells the bride that she has become a whore, and that she is even more abominable than her *"sisters,"* the infamous *"Samaria"* and *"Sodom"* (vv. 46-58).

This is highly sexualized and highly controversial language, then and now. It is intended to be shocking. Often missed in the sexual nature of the language is that the core deadly sins of Israel are those of pride, gluttony and sloth. Too much *"food"* and *"ease"* has led to a moral laziness. And this uncaring and bored sloth has led to a lustful negligence and pagan dalliances. It has broken the heart of God, the scorned lover of his chosen bride.

Why would Ezekiel use such extreme language? Because he was dealing with extreme entitlement. Jerusalem thought of herself as the holy city, the chosen people. She forgot that her ancestry was nothing special, and that her status as "chosen" was conferred on her by a gracious God, not inherent in her bloodlines. Entitlement is always a step away from haughtiness. And the haughty are never able to partner with God. Never.

A leader watching Ezekiel's example may think twice before using such sexually-charged language. What we can learn, though, is that moral complacency must be met by verbal challenge that is equally intense. Leaders don't use powerful metaphors for simple shock value. But when the patient's heart is flat-lining, powerful shocking is in order. Entrenched complacency and entitlement must be countered by extreme words.

John P. Chandler

EZEKIEL 17

"Will he succeed? Can one escape who does such things? Can he break the covenant and yet escape?" – **Ezekiel 17:15**

Praying the Prophets

Another in his series of allegorical sermons, the prophet here tells a "*riddle*" (v. 1) that interprets the political intrigue of kings Zedekiah and Jehoiachin from 598 B.C. until exile in 586. Beyond realpolitik, royal deception was not simple strategic miscalculation. The kings' deception instead was a deeply spiritual matter, an offense to God, and a cause of the fall of Judah. Ezekiel mentions "*covenant*" six times and "*oath*" four times in the allegory. The problem is royal lying. Deception and dishonesty in governance has brought on judgment from God.

The allegory is clear: the moral, spiritual, and political realms are inseparable. Broken political promises lead to rebellions of all sorts. When kings lie, they rebel against God and foment rebellion among nations.

Someone recently described to me how her parents – pious but deceptive people – taught her and her siblings to use the word "fib" instead of "lie." It was an attempt to soften their dishonesty and justify the practice. We will even play word games to skirt around our breaking of the ninth commandment (Exodus 20:16)!

Writer Dan Ariely asserts that all of us lie on some level. Ezekiel preaches that this is a terrible idea. Leaders who break promises with those they lead, beware: you are messing with God. And like a "*great eagle*" (v. 3) swooping over cedars, God will pluck those twigs.

John P. Chandler

EZEKIEL 18

"What do you mean by repeating this proverb concerning the land of Israel, "The parents have eaten sour grapes and the children's teeth are set on edge"? As I live, says the Lord God, this proverb shall no more be used by you in Israel."
– Ezekiel 18:2-3

In Ezekiel 18, the prophet does the classic pastoral work of "afflicting the comfortable and comforting the afflicted." Cynicism is so rampant among exiles that it is captured in a proverb of conventional wisdom: "*the parents have eaten sour grapes and the children's teeth are set on edge.*" The die is cast, the game is fixed, the outcome is pre-determined ... so says the prevailing conventional wisdom.

But much of what a leader does is refute conventional wisdom. And with lawyer-like precision, Ezekiel builds a case for moral accountability and the possibility of change. To those seeking to evade personal responsibility by blaming others (their parents, previous generations) for their problems, the prophet is harsh: buck up, look in the mirror, and take responsibility. The mess you are in is no one's fault but your own.

However, to those who are beaten down into hopelessness about their situation, Ezekiel turns this same message on its head. We are not, he says, pre-determined by others to fail and flail. "*It is only the person who sins that shall die*" (v. 4). If we "*turn from our transgressions*" and get "*a new heart and a new spirit,*" then we can "*turn and live*" (vv. 30-32). We are not condemned to futility by the sins of others. Change is possible. The future is open. And we can do something about it. You are not helpless and hopeless. With God, all things are possible!

Again, Ezekiel models the leader's work of countering cynicism and conventional public wisdom. That he does so by simultaneously holding people to account and giving them an avenue of hope is an example for all of us who have the opportunity to influence.

EZEKIEL 20

"As I entered into judgment with your ancestors in the wilderness of the land of Egypt, so I will enter into judgment with you, says the Lord God." – Ezekiel 20:36

In the middle of national crisis and turmoil, everyone is compelled to understand what is going on. The impulse to interpret suffering is as old as Job and his friends. Often, people frame this in terms of figuring out who to blame for trouble (Ezekiel 18).

In chapter 20, Ezekiel interprets current life within the larger framework of a bigger and older story. Judah's current situation, he says, is not an anomaly. It is an echo of a much older story. At least three times – Egypt, the first wilderness generation, and the second wilderness generation – the people of God lived a pattern:

- ➣ God's act of grace to his people;

- ➣ God's requirement of their response;

- ➣ Their unfaithfulness;

- ➣ God's warning, then reprieve;

- ➣ Threat of punishment, and exaction of that punishment.

"This," says the prophet, "is exactly what is going on right now. Our culture is experiencing the execution of divine judgment." As harsh as that message must sound to those who hear it, it's ultimately good news. There is a pattern and moral coherence in the universe! And Ezekiel's work is to name it.

The work of the leader is to locate what seem like random episodes within larger patterns. Leaders help people see that apparently unexplainable situations are not glitches, but well-worn grooves in the larger way.

Prayer: *God, grant me the wisdom to see the connectedness of things today. Give me understanding and insight to interpret episodes as part of patterns and to help others make sense of what is going on within them, between and among them, and around them. And please do this work of revelation within my own heart as well. In the name of Jesus Christ, Amen.*

EZEKIEL 22

THE FIVE P'S

"And I sought for anyone among them who would repair the wall and standing in the breach before me on behalf of the land, so that I would not destroy it; but I found no one."
– Ezekiel 22:30

Ezekiel is presenting what some commentators call a "catalogue of crime." He is looking to make sense of Exile, to interpret the incredible suffering of God's people. With sword and fire (chapter 21) and now as a *"smelter"* (vv. 18ff), God judges the moral degeneration that inevitably follows from idolatry (vv. 3ff). Judah has violated the Holiness Code (Leviticus 17-26); interesting, Ezekiel adds to that ancient list her current economic crimes: *"bribery, usury, and extortion"* (v. 12).

The prophet's hardest words are for the people of influence who did not, like Abraham interceding to God for sparing Sodom (Genesis 18:22-33), *"stand in the breach on behalf of the land."* Leadership failed because it did not intervene. These failed leaders (vv. 25-29) were the "five P's":

1. Princes – nobles of wealth who failed to use their resources;

2. Priests – keepers of moral tradition who did not speak at violations of ethics and taboo;

3. Politicians – those who traded public service for personal gain;

4. Prophets – those who spoke falsehood in the name of God; and

5. People – the general population who allowed outrageous leadership to continue *"without redress"* (v. 29).

And who is affected most by failed leadership? A sixth "P": the poor and needy, the *"alien"* who suffers *"extortion"* (v. 29). These are the people who get hurt most when leaders fail.

God's judgment on a corrupt society smelts all in it. But the hardest judgments are reserved for leaders – the five P's – who could most have stood to do something about it. God, help us.

John P. Chandler 215

EZEKIEL 24

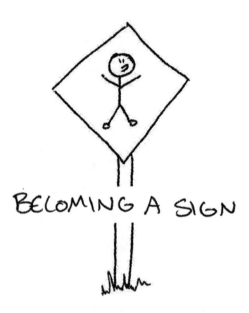

"Mortal, with one blow I am about to take away from you the delight of your eyes; yet you shall not mourn or weep, nor shall your tears run down ... Thus Ezekiel shall be a sign to you ..." **– Ezekiel 24:16, 24**

Ezekiel has cajoled and threatened. He has demonstrated his warnings with symbolic (and sometimes strange) actions. He has warned Jerusalem with straightforward threats from the Almighty. He has even composed something like drinking ditties – the "song of the pot" in 24:1-13 – to make his point.

But now, on the precise date of the beginning of the siege of Jerusalem (January 15, 588 B.C.), Ezekiel's very life itself will embody his message. His wife, the *"delight of your eyes,"* will die that very day. He will predict it in the morning, and it will happen in the evening. Though deeply grieved, he is not to mourn openly. And that stiff upper lip in the face of unspeakable loss is a sign of things to come for his audience. Jerusalem, God's beloved delight and *"heart's affection"* (v. 25), is also about to be sacked and die. And there will be no time to mourn her.

Obviously, leaders do whatever they can to get their message across. One thing Ezekiel's experience points toward is the inevitable participation of the leader in the experience of those whom s/he leads. When we lead, it's personal – deeply so. And God uses even our deepest suffering and personal tragedy as part of how we connect with and communicate our mission.

Isaiah had his "suffering servant," and Ezekiel lost his beloved wife. Ultimately God himself would come in the person of Jesus Christ and give his very life on a cross as a ransom for many. When the message is invaluable, our full immersion and participation in it is required.

EZEKIEL 25

INTERNATIONAL JUSTICE

*"Because with unending hostilities the Philistines acted
in vengeance, and with malice of heart took revenge in
destruction; therefore thus says the Lord God, I will stretch
out my hand against the Philistines, cut off the Cherethites,
and destroy the rest of the seacoast."* – **Ezekiel 25:15**

Carefully placed between the siege (chapter 24) and fall (chapter 32) of Jerusalem, Ezekiel's seven "oracles against the nations" are a harbinger of hope to Israel, because they assert that every nation will get what it deserves from God. These seven nations have been complicit co-conspirators in Babylon's overthrow of Judah. They seem to have gotten away with (or even profited from) it. But Ezekiel spends eight chapters saying, "Not so." Judah won't be the only nation judged.

Such "execration texts" that promise God's future comeuppance to other nations are found in ten of the fifteen biblical prophets. One tenth of all biblical prophetic writing is devoted to oracles against other nations. The practice famously continues into the New Testament, most notably in the book of Revelation's pronouncements against "*Babylon*" as a cipher for the Roman Empire. We have to ask why Ezekiel (and other prophets) gives such a dominant space to the warning of certain accountability for the rivals of the people of God.

Surely part of it is because neighborhood rivalries are fiercest. But beyond that, in the midst of experiencing accountability for her sins, broken Judah has to hear that <u>every</u> nation will be judged by God for its deeds. It is good news to remember that no one gets away with murder. The universe is still morally sensible. Even nations that seem to have escaped the Babylonian scourge will face a more significant (divine) reckoning one day. Our deeds matter. No nation, despite its current ruling status, is above and beyond the judgment of God. None can act with moral impunity and evade justice.

American slaves used to speak of heaven and hell not simply as "pie in the sky," but as a way of celebrating the final justice of God. Hell is not a happy thought, unless people are currently getting away with murder unpunished and need to be held to account. The justice of God means we <u>all</u> will stand before the judgment seat of God. Our behavior here bears on the judgment there. The God of the Bible doesn't simply relate to his chosen people. Whether they know and accept it or not, this God of justice relates to <u>all</u>.

EZEKIEL 26-28

ESCALATING TO BIBLICAL PROPORTIONS

"For thus says the Lord God: When I make you a city laid waste, like cities that are not inhabited, when I bring up the deep over you, and the great waters cover you, then I will thrust you down with those who descend into the Pit, to the people of long ago, and I will make you live in the world below, among primeval ruins ...." – **Ezekiel 26:19-2**

Ezekiel continues his long section of oracles against the nations (chapters 25-32) with seven broadsides against the nation Tyre. Tyre has been salivating at the fall of Jerusalem, a commercial competitor. While four of the prophet's retorts to Tyre are unremarkable, three catch our attention because Ezekiel frames the situation in mythic language. Tyre's fall will be like:

- A descent into *"the Pit"* (26:20);

- The fall of *"Eden"* (27:11ff);

- A Noah flood (28:9); and

- The undoing of ordered creation into the *"prickling briers"* and *"piercing thorns"* of chaos (28:24).

In short, the prophet, using mythic descriptions, escalates the situation into the proverbial "biblical proportions."

Too often, leaders speak of what we face in mythic language. Thus football games become "war," and political enemies become "an axis of evil." This can be either strikingly foolish or do real harm. A good leader won't make that mistake.

But neither will a good leader refrain from speaking in mythic language regarding matters of ultimate concern. There is a time and place when the heart and soul of those we lead is at stake. In that day, the language of heaven and hell, chaos and creation, flood and garden captures something mere prose cannot. Leaders have to know when to frame and escalate a situation into a matter of biblical proportions.

John P. Chandler   221

EZEKIEL 29–32

DON'T TRUST THE UNTRUSTWORTHY

"Then all the inhabitants of Egypt shall know that I am the Lord because you were a staff of reed to the house of Israel; when they grasped you with the hand, you broke, and tore all their shoulders; and when they leaned on you, you broke and made all their legs unsteady." – Ezekiel 29:6-7

Ezekiel's seventh oracle against the nations (chapters 25-32) itself contains seven oracles, and is thus the climax and focus of his word of judgment. His bitterest words are for Israel's archrival, Egypt. In the Bible, "*Egypt*" is beyond geography; it is code for proud nations opposed to the people of God. Egypt is the devil's "Duke" to God's "Carolina!"

The prophet's words condemn both Israel's foolishness for relying on Egypt, and also Egypt's pride and unreliability. Once again, the people of God have again leaned on a human king (Pharaoh) rather than God as their King. Now, not only will they pay the price through Exile, but the toweringly proud Egyptians will be brought low. Egypt will be a crocodile thrown on the banks and fed to the birds (chapter 30), a great cedar chopped down (chapter 31), suffering the fate of the unburied war-dead (chapter 32). Imagine a failed state saying this to a nation whose pyramids still stand today! But Ezekiel includes many dates to verify his predictions of Egypt's fall. And fall they did.

For a nation, this oracle is a warning against elevating the power of a state above the sovereignty of God. For an individual leader, it can be taken as a warning not to rely on unreliable would-be allies. If you lie down with dogs, you'll wake up with flees. Don't trust the untrustworthy. Don't lean on a flimsy *"reed"* when you need a sturdier staff. If you dine with devil, you better have a long spoon. Israel made that mistake nationally. A wise leader won't repeat it.

Exercise: *Are you relying on someone who is not trustworthy? If so, ask why – and be prepared to move forward without them.*

John P. Chandler   223

EZEKIEL 33

PREACHER'S LAMENT

"To them you are like a singer of love songs, one who has a beautiful voice and plays well on an instrument; they hear what you say, but they will not do it." – Ezekiel 33:32

After nearly seven years as a *"sentinel"* who *"blows the trumpet and warns the people"* (v. 3), Ezekiel's role has transitioned. No longer is he the prophet of judgment and personal accountability to the overconfident. Now, he becomes a pastor to the broken. And for the next fifteen years, he will try to speak words of restoration and hope to the remnants of a destroyed nation. The work of tearing down the old is always only half of rebuilding the new!

The leadership problems Ezekiel faces, though, remain the same: people will come to hear from him *"what the word is that comes from the Lord."* They *"hear your words, but they will not obey them"* (vv. 30f). His speeches are well-attended and widely praised. They just aren't obeyed.

What leader doesn't understand this? Hearers complimented Ezekiel that he was *"like a singer of love songs, one who has a beautiful voice and plays well on an instrument"* (v. 32). But they didn't respond with action to his words. Jesus would similarly lament the low response rate to his words: his *"seed"* fell on rocky, shallow or thorny *"soil,"* and was only occasionally received fruitfully (Matthew 13:1-23).

If Jesus and Ezekiel experienced this, we should expect no different. For a leader, here's a reality check: stirring rhetoric may titilate, but doesn't necessarily motivate. As coaches know, stirring halftime speeches don't win ballgames. Our job isn't completed with artful words, but is validated in listener response. Leadership effectiveness is not finally measured off the lips of the speaker, but in the ear – and actions – of the hearer.

John P. Chandler

EZEKIEL 34

PRINCE, NOT KING

"I will set up over them one shepherd, my servant David, and he shall feed them: he shall feed them and be their shepherd. And I, the Lord, will be their God, and my servant David shall be prince among them; I, the Lord, have spoken."
– Ezekiel 34:23-24

Ezekiel's pastoral work of restoring a broken people continues in chapter 34, where he picks up the old biblical metaphor of the leader as shepherd (first used in Genesis 49:24, and most famously used in the twenty-third Psalm). His distinction between good and bad shepherd/leaders rehearses typical contrasts of self-interested versus servant leaders.

But Ezekiel launches a trajectory to be explored in the rest of the New Testament when he announces that God will soon send a final (messianic) leader. This "*one shepherd*," from the line of David, will be a "*prince*" of God the "*king*." The Exile itself was the final failure a nation who wanted to have a human king in order to be like other nations (1 Samuel 8). According to Ezekiel, what God's broken people need is not another king, but a prince who leads as a servant of God the king. This leader leads not by exploiting his position or power, but by doing the will of his heavenly King.

This is the trajectory picked up by Jesus, who described his final work as a prince in this way: "*I am the good shepherd. The good shepherd lays down his life for the sheep*" (John 10:11). Leaders who follow in the way of Jesus, and of Ezekiel's good shepherd, lead through laying down their lives as princes or princesses, not as kings. We lead even as we serve our King.

EZEKIEL 36

EDEN RESTORED

"And they will say, "This land that was desolate has become like the garden of Eden; and the waste and desolate and ruined towns are now inhabited and fortified. Then the nations that are left all around you shall know that I, the Lord, have rebuilt the ruined places, and replanted that which was desolate; I, the Lord, have spoken, and I will do it."
– Ezekiel 36:35-36

Ezekiel is speaking to people who have been deconstructed at every level of existence by the conquering Babylonians. Socially, they have been decimated. Jerusalem and Judah lie in ruins. Theologically, surrounding nations "*taunt*" and "*profane*" the God of Israel (v. 20). The reputation and dignity of Yahweh is in tatters because of the sorry state of his people.

Because the destruction is so complete, the prophet's vision of restoration has to be equally comprehensive. Thus Ezekiel describes a work of salvation of Eden-like proportions. It will involve the transformation of:

> ➣ individuals: "*A new heart I will give you, and a new spirit I will put within you*" (v. 26);

> ➣ society: "*so shall the ruined towns be filled with flocks of people*" (v. 38); and

> ➣ nature: "*I will make the fruit of the tree and the produce of the field abundant, so that you may never again suffer the disgrace of famine among the nations*" (v. 30).

As with the rest of the Bible, the coming salvation, promised as a work of God, is a divine gift of transformation, not escape. It is the work of salvation <u>for</u> the world, not <u>from</u> the world.

The work of a leader is to proclaim a vision whose scale of hope matches the crisis at hand. It is to understand and work in concert with the divine vision of the renewal of Eden, the restoration of all things that God intends.

John P. Chandler   229

EZEKIEL 37

RESURRECTION AND REUNION FOR WITNESS

"My dwelling place shall be with them; and I will be their God, and they shall be my people. Then the nations shall know that I the Lord sanctify Israel, when my sanctuary is among them forevermore." – Ezekiel 37:27-28

Ezekiel's most famous vision (the valley of the dry bones in verses 1-14) is combined in chapter 37 with an oracle about two sticks becoming one (vv. 15-28). Jewish interpreters of this passage have focused on these words as a forecast of reunion of the twelve tribes – complete with Law, Promised Land, Davidic king, restored covenant, and central sanctuary (vv. 22-26). Later Christian interpreters saw this vision as anticipating the doctrine of resurrection of the dead. In either case, it is wholly an initiative of God to speak life as a divine gift to a broken, dispersed, and hopeless people.

But life is given by God toward what end? These are visions about a work of God toward corporate (not individual) resurrection. And what purpose would resurrection and reunion serve? Ezekiel says that they move toward establishing a *"dwelling place"* or *"sanctuary"* that bears witness to the nations about who God is and how he wants to relate to people (vv. 27f). God brings life and unity to his people because they have a role to fill in the world. God's people are to give a picture of the ultimate purposes of the Lord in the world and in history.

Leaders who use these pictures of resurrection and reunion should do so with this larger framework in mind. These visions have long been applied by Bible students wishing to encourage dead or dying companies, families, nations. *"Can these bones live?"* And the visions do speak of the hope of God doing a new thing. But God doesn't simply want to breathe life into dead bones as a parlor trick. It is because that revived body has work to do in the world, and that work has to do with how the world sees the God who gives life. God gives resurrection and reunion because God wants us to be living examples of who he is and how he is at work in the world among his people.

John P. Chandler   231

EZEKIEL 40-42

THE CENTER OF THE UNIVERSE

"In the twenty-fifth year of our exile ... the hand of the Lord was upon me, and he brought me there. He brought me, in visions of God, to the land of Israel, and set me down upon a very high mountain, on which was a structure like a city to the south." – Ezekiel 40:1-2

A quarter-century after Israel was demolished, the prophet and pastor Ezekiel passes along a vision to his people for the future. It is Eden, Sinai, and Zion combined. Its location is a *"very high mountain"* – a place of divine revelation. And it is a *"structure like a city"* – a picture of the ideal community. According to this vision of hope, the ultimate center of the universe is a temple.

The specific measurements of the temple are listed in almost maniacal detail, because it is a place where careful and precise attention is given to proper ritual life. In this *"city"* the profane and sacred are separate. Here, every aspect of life, personal and social, revolves around our proper relationship to a holy God and to right relationships with each other and the world. No wonder Revelation 21-22 (the climax of the Bible) picks up this imagery and pictures the final destiny of humanity as life in a *"new Jerusalem,"* a city descended to earth from heaven, in which there is vitality, beauty, worship, and the fulfillment of God's intentions for the world he created.

Ezekiel sees the End of all things, the final vision of the beloved community, as captured in life revolving around worship of God. For him, the kingdom of God is no longer historical Israel; it is a people properly oriented around this worship. At the center of the universe is no longer a nation, but a temple. And those who live in the heart of reality give their lives, first and most, to the worship of almighty God. Our ultimate work is a liturgy.

And like Ezekiel, a good leader today never lets us forget this final vision, for it shapes the way we do everything between here and there.

EZEKIEL 43

"When these days are over, then from the eight day onward the priests shall offer upon the altar your burnt offerings and your offerings of well-being; and I will accept you, says the Lord God." – Ezekiel 43:27

Ezekiel's final vision of hope for his exiled people is the return of the "*glory of the Lord*" (v. 4) in their midst. God has been preparing a new city for his people to occupy while they suffered in a distant land – something God continues to do until this day (Revelation 21-22). At the center of the new city will be a new temple. And at the center of the temple will be the practices of proper sacrifice. When these places and practices are properly centered, God's glory will shine, and holiness will abound in the earth.

Jerusalem had been destroyed by Babylon, God's instrument, because "*temple*" and "*kings*" had become too cozy (vv. 7-9). No more! The temple will no longer be polluted by being used as an instrument of the palace. For a new city to work well, church must not be contaminated as a simple arm of the crown or state. In the new temple, God alone is King.

And what happens in this new temple and city? Primarily, according to Ezekiel, what happens is <u>sacrifice</u>. Centuries later (70 A.D.), the Romans would finally destroy again the temple in Jerusalem, and Jews and Christians would have to internalize the practice of sacrifice (Romans 12:1, "*offer your bodies as living sacrifices to God, holy and acceptable*"). For Ezekiel, elaborate instructions about how the people are to sacrifice are necessary (vv. 18-26) because his message is singular and clear: the purpose of a new people in a new temple in a new city is for us to learn how to relate rightly to God, to each other, and to the world by learning how to sacrifice well.

This still holds true, and a leader never lets his or her people forget it. Greatness and "*well-being*" comes through rightly ordered practices of sacrifice. When we learn to model sacrifice well, a new city gets put back together, and a vision of hope for the world emerges.

John P. Chandler   235

EZEKIEL 44

REQUIREMENTS FOR REPLACEMENT LEADERS

"It is they who shall enter my sanctuary, it is they who shall approach my table, to minister to me, and they shall keep my charge." **– Ezekiel 44:16**

In the new city and new temple of Ezekiel's hopeful vision for his people, there will be new leaders. Out with the old leaders, who had been complicit in the moral degradation of the people that led to their fall. In with the new spiritual leaders, whose personal character and habits would authenticate and legitimate their spiritual leadership.

Certainly there is a ritual and tribal back-story here (Levite vs. Zadokite). But beyond that lies the prophet's description of how replacement leaders must build their work on a foundation of personal moral rectitude. For Ezekiel, these are the critical components for a moral leader charged with rebuilding on a corrupt legacy:

1. Personal habits – Ezekiel declared that not only the person's physical public appearance matter (vv. 17-20, clothing and hairstyle!), but also the leader's relationship with alcohol (v. 21), diet (vv. 29ff), and his marital status (v. 22) are also fair game.

2. Moral teaching – *"They shall teach my people the difference between the holy and the common, and show them how to distinguish between the unclean and the clean"* (v. 23).

3. Sound spiritual judgment – *"In a controversy, they shall act as judges, and they shall decide it according to my judgments"* (v. 24).

4. Financial integrity – *"This shall be their inheritance: I am their inheritance; and you shall give them no holding in Israel; I am their holding"* (v. 28).

Dismiss if you will the arcane ritual peculiarities of Israel's clergy. Ezekiel's prophetic pronouncements about the character of replacement leaders still rings true: to lead others spiritually, new leaders entering a new (rebuilt) city have to live moral lives worth emulating.

John P. Chandler 237

EZEKIEL 46

LEADERS WITH PEOPLE

"When the people of the land come before the Lord at the appointed festivals ... they shall not return by way of the gate by which they entered, but shall go out straight ahead. When they come in, the prince shall come in with them; and when they go out, he shall go out." – Ezekiel 46:9-10

Ezekiel's final long vision (chapters 40-48) to his broken people is a hopeful vision of a holy community. Holiness is a well-structured life oriented around God at the center of all things. Such re-centering impacts calendar (46:1ff), land, (45:1ff), economics (45:10-12), and even diet (46:21-24). A new and holy city is a community of new time and new space.

And it is led by a new kind of leader. No longer is such a holy city governed by kings and high priests, for they were complicit in the contamination that got everyone in a mess in the first place. Now, Ezekiel sees the leaders as a *"prince,"* whose role seems to be chief worshiper. This worship occurs both at *"festivals"* (v. 11) and *"morning by morning"* (vv. 13-15); worship is both daily and seasonal. And the separation of prince and people is minimized; now the prince *"shall come in with them"* to worship. Interestingly, when prince is with people and they enter the temple, they go out of a different gate than the one by which they entered. Everyone's direction is new once they encounter God in the temple.

Ezekiel's vision of the new prince-leader helped to set the stage for the coming of Jesus as the ultimate model of leadership. Incarnate Jesus would come as "the Word became flesh" who "lived among us," and who would be "full of grace and truth" (John 1:14). Finally, we would understand from this "Prince of Peace" that leaders are not to be segregated away from those whom they lead. Their greatness comes from their fundamental willingness to lead <u>with</u> people. Ezekiel foreshadows that ideal leaders will *"come in"* and *"go out"* with people in a new order of life and a new city.

Exercise: *Which arena of your life — your calendar, possessions, money or diet — needs to step toward holiness? How can you work toward holiness by being <u>with</u> people and not apart from them?*

John P. Chandler   239

EZEKIEL 47-48

RIVER
AND
TREE

"On the banks, on both sides of the river, there will grow all kinds of trees for food. Their leaves will not wither nor their fruit fail, but they will bear fresh fruit every month, because the water for them flows from the sanctuary. Their fruit will be for food, and their leaves for healing." **– Ezekiel 47:12**

In Ezekiel's day, in the words of scholars Bruce Vawter and Leslie Hoppe,

> "... the Athenians were building the Acropolis and the Mayans were building their temples. Aesop was spinning his fables and Lao-tse was sharing his wisdom. The sixth century before Christ was an age of burgeoning culture throughout the world" (Vawter and Hoppe, *Ezekiel: A New Heart*, p. 213).

Ezekiel's contribution of hope to his war-torn and shattered people in exile is a picture of a mythic city and temple. Like Eden in Genesis 1-2 and the Holy City in Revelation 21-22, this hopeful sanctuary-city is marked by a "*river*" and "*trees.*"

The river, ever-deepening (47:3-5), gives life even to a Dead Sea: "*Wherever the river goes, every living creature that swarms will live*" (47:9). The trees will provide "*fruit for food*" and "*leaves for healing.*" (No wonder followers of Jesus proclaim that this life-tree is the cross!) In a city marked by River and Tree, nature is restored, the Genesis 3 curse is reversed, and paradise is realized: "*And the name of the city from that time on shall be, The Lord is here.*" (48:35)

River and trees: movement and fixedness ... ever-changing newness and life-giving stability ... vitality and fruitfulness – Ezekiel has captured a picture of what a city, people, and the world can look like when redeemed by God. It is a grand, sweeping vision of the way things are meant by God to be in the world. And every leader in every culture gives voice toward moving people toward dwelling in this new city, the city of God, a city fed by ever-deepening fresh streams and nourished by fresh fruit in the shade of great trees.

John P. Chandler

DANIEL 1

NEGOTIATING CULTURE

"But Daniel resolved that he would not defile himself with the royal rations of food and wine; so he asked the palace master to allow him not to defile himself. Now God allowed Daniel to receive favor and compassion from the palace master." – Daniel 1:8-9

Spanning life under the rule of many foreign empires (Babylonian, Persian, Greek, etc.) and bridging the Bible's prophetic and apocalyptic responses of faith, the book of Daniel describes how a wise and godly leader is to respond ethically when s/he is not in charge. Like earlier biblical stories of Joseph and Esther, Daniel 1 is an overture which describes the challenges of negotiating how to live and lead from the second chair.

Young Daniel and his renamed associates are minor associates in the royal court who try to remain faithful to God. To do so, they accept the royal education, but reject the royal diet and the compromises it entails. As a result, they are found to be *"ten times better"* as advisors to the king (v. 20).

H. Richard Niebuhr's most famous work, *Christ and Culture,* outlines a history of how Christianity has responded to culture with five dominant viewpoints:

- **Christ against Culture**

- **Christ of Culture**

- **Christ above Culture**

- **Christ and Culture in Paradox**

- **Christ Transforming Culture**

Niebuhr helpfully captures the nuanced range of responses in the Bible as to when we are to work <u>with</u> the prevailing ethos of our age, and when to reject it starkly.

What is clear in Daniel, though, is that any leader in an environment hostile, indifferent, or compromising to our faith must learn how to carry faith vigorously into the heartland of all that opposes this faith. For him, it was, "Take the education, reject the diet."

We have to say No to compromises both subtle and great that would blur our mission and co-opt our identity. We may be forcibly re-named by our oppressor, and may actually benefit from the education they provide us. But there is also a day to reject their "*royal diet*" and to maintain our clearest and first identity: as ambassadors of a greater King than whatever king happens to be "in charge" that day.

Praying the Prophets

DANIEL 2

ACCESS TO WISDOM ... IN THE FACE OF MYSTERY

"(Daniel) told them to seek mercy from the God of heaven concerning this mystery, so that Daniel and his companions with the rest of the wise men of Babylon might not perish. Then the mystery was revealed to Daniel in a vision of the night, and Daniel blessed the God of heaven."
– Daniel 2:18-19

Like Joseph in an Egyptian prison (Genesis 39-41), Daniel is a man of wisdom, without position or title, living in the shadow of a king who is about to embark on genocide because he cannot interpret a troubling dream. The king is baffled, the court sages cannot read his confused, royal mind, and he is about to break bad on them for it. Daniel is but a mere young courtier, an exiled foreigner, without title, about to be wiped out in the greater flood of the king's rage. (The king is an anti-leader: when you can't solve a problem, just kill someone!)

But Daniel leads from the second chair. He is confident that *"there is a God in heaven who reveals mysteries"* (v. 28), and it's not the gods of the empire. He humbly begins to *"seek mercy,"* and prays to *"the God of heaven."* (By the way, which God to whom you pray matters; it isn't that "prayer changes things" but prayer to the God of heaven, the particular God Yahweh that can change things.) And in the face of a baffling crisis, *"mystery was revealed."* Daniel immediately *"blessed the God of heaven"* and breaks out in a humble psalm of praise. The king is convinced: *"Truly, your God is God of gods and Lord of kings and a revealer of mysteries!"* (v. 47). The king settles, crisis abates, the court survives, and Daniel is promoted.

This is a story to remind leaders that even in the face of seemingly insolvable mysteries and from positions of where we don't have power to engineer change, we are not without power. We do not have to strike out in rage. We have access to wisdom and interpretation in the face of mystery. When we humbly call on the right God, *"the God of heaven,"* the true ruler Yahweh, we can lead wisely and well even in situations of exile and crisis.

DANIEL 3

OUR
PRE- COMMITMENTS

"Shadrach, Meshach, and Abednego answered the king, "O Nebuchadnezzar, we have no need to present a defense to you in this matter." – Daniel 3:16

Praying the Prophets

Inevitably, during political campaigns, I am disappointed in how allegiances to a political party trump the ability of some Christians to prioritize their decisions as citizens through the lenses of their faith. Many seem unwilling to suspend their prior held perspectives – what I call their "pre-commitments" – to a partisan perspective. And these pre-commitments override and preclude any open or new thinking through the lens of biblical faith.

Daniel 3 is a story of pre-commitments, good and bad. The king, Nebuchadnezzar, is so "all-in" that all should bow to the statue of himself, that his *"face was distorted"* with rage when loyal servants wouldn't bow (vv. 13, 19). Holding the wrong pre-commitments is no virtue; it is hard-headedness at best and egomania at worst. The Nazis were pre-committed.

On the other hand, neither do the three friends of Daniel – Shadrach, Meshach, and Abednego – have to wrestle with this decree. They are pre-committed toward loyalty to the God of the Bible who will brook no idols. They don't have to pray about it. They are ready to burn in the furnace before breaking their pre-commitment to faithfulness.

In this Holocaust story, the faithful servants are rescued from the fiery furnace. In other Holocausts, the servants die. But martyrdom is preferable to apostasy. And when we have the right pre-commitments, then live or die, we are a force and testimony to a world that wavers.

A leader thus not only has to encourage unswerving devotion, but to guide people toward devotion to the proper pre-commitments.

Exercise: *Name one proper and one improper pre-commitment in your life – and ask God to respond to those.*

John P. Chandler

DANIEL 4

"While the words were still in the king's mouth, a voice
came from heaven: "O King Nebuchadnezzar, to you it is
declared: The kingdom has departed from you! You shall be
driven away from human society, and your dwelling shall
be with the animals of the field. You shall be made to eat
grass like oxen, and seven times shall pass over you, until you
have learned that the Most High has sovereignty over the
kingdom of mortals and gives it to whom he will."
– Daniel 4:31-32

Praying the Prophets

Leaders: forget what you've been taught about the power of devotion, prayer, and dreaming!

We have already learned from Daniel that devotion itself doesn't change things, but devotion to the right God does. Prayer itself doesn't change things, but prayer to the Most High God does. And in chapter 4, Daniel reminds us that "dreaming" in and of itself doesn't determine outcomes. Human leaders may cast vision and have dreams, but God has a dream, too – and that dream happens to matter.

King Nebuchadnezzar, legendary builder, was dreaming large, *"living at ease"* and *"prospering in my palace"* (v. 4). He dreams of himself as the great world tree planted and ruling at the center of the universe. But when he is helplessly asleep, he is given an unwanted dream that the tree is cut down (v. 14). Daniel interprets it for him straight-up: the dreamer king shall be cut off from human society (vv. 25, 32), the ultimate punishment. The creation story of Eden is (for the king) put in reverse, and he reverts to behaving like an animal (*"eat grass like oxen,"* v. 25). He descends into madness and (unlike the rich fool of Luke 12:15-21) escapes with his life. Then, *"my reason returned to me"* (v. 34), whereupon he wisely begins to *"praise and extol and honor the King of Heaven"* (v. 37).

Say all you will about the power of vision-casting and sharing your dream. But unless our dreams line up with God's dreams for the world, it can be a train wreck!

Exercise: *Obviously, you can't control your dreams. But humbly ask God to speak to you through dreams in ways that confirm, confront, and compel you.*

DANIEL 5

"Then Daniel answered in the presence of the king, "Let your gifts be for yourself, or give your rewards to someone else! Nevertheless I will read the writing to the king and let him know the interpretation." – Daniel 5:17

Praying the Prophets

Daniel 5 is the story of a prophet who has to bring a very blunt and unhappy word to the powers-that-be. King Belshazzar – whether on drunken whim or deliberate challenge – is conducting a drunk-fest and using the sacred vessels of the Jerusalem temple. It is hard to fathom which of his sins is greatest: pride, stupidity, or blasphemy.

In the midst of this, he sees the proverbial "handwriting on the wall." The finger of God which inscribed the Ten Commandments inscribes words, and no court magician can interpret. (These inept people were on staff?!) Daniel is remembered as a man of wisdom from generations past and is brought in with the promise of purple clothes, gold chains, and to *"rank third in the kingdom"* (v. 16) if he can interpret. The given interpretation is short, sweet, and accurate: your days are numbered. And so the king was killed that very night.

While Daniel is promoted, as were other biblical prophets (Joseph in Genesis 41, Mordecai in the book of Esther), a striking note for leaders is that he said his word from God independent of desire for reward or fear of punishment. Keep your gifts, or give them away – but here is the straight truth from God that you are not going to want to hear!

Who is the true leader here, king Belshazzar or the prophet Daniel?! Leaders can't be bought. They are not swayed by *"gifts."* They say what they are charged to speak independent of offers of reward or fear of reprisal.

Exercise: *Are you motivated by fear of punishment? Desire for reward? Or something else? Ponder what spurs you to action. And ask God to make you wary of bribes and their effects.*

DANIEL 6

HOW PRAYER WORKS

"Although Daniel knew that the document had been signed, he continued to go to his house, which had windows in its upper room open toward Jerusalem, and to get down on his knees three times a day to pray to his God and praise him, just as he had done previously. The conspirators came and found Daniel praying and seeking mercy before his God."
– Daniel 6:10-11

Praying the Prophets

Prayer can get you in trouble! (Ask Daniel, and ask Jesus.) Refusing to pray to the state and instead praying to the God of Israel caused Daniel to be thrown into a lion's den. He was saved through a combination of God's deliverance, a king's help, and his own faithfulness.

It is instructive to look phrase by phrase at the shape of Daniel's prayerful faithfulness. In vv. 10-11, he:

- Went to an *"upper room"* in *"his house"* – having a designated place to pray that was totally integrated with his daily life;

- Prayed *"toward Jerusalem"* – symbol of hope and the future, which shaped his posture of expectancy;

- Got *"down on his knees"* – indicating the fundamental humility necessary for effective prayer;

- Did so *"three times a day"* – fashioned as part of a daily disciplined routine and not flung upwards only in crisis; and

- Consisted of *"praise"* and *"seeking mercy before his God."*

The great irony of the story of Daniel in the lion's den is that while many thought the king's laws were immutable, it turns out that his rules were quite temporal and powerless in face of God's rule and reign. And the good news is that we have access to God's rule and reign – in part now and one day fully – through faithful prayer.

DANIEL 7

THE UNCREATED CREATOR

"As for these four great beasts, four kings shall arise out of the earth. But the holy ones of the Most High shall receive the kingdom and possess the kingdom forever – forever and ever." – Daniel 7:17-18

The Bible describes two categories of "being." It is persistently careful to distinguish the created realm from the Uncreated Creator who made all that is in it. To confuse the two in any way is idolatry. And throughout human history, people in power have confused the two.

Daniel 7 describes four human kingdoms (the Babylonians, Medes, Persians, and Greeks) as *"beasts"* arising out of the *"sea"* (v. 2, a classic biblical symbol of chaos). They are beastly because they:

> ❧ *"speak words against the Most High";*

> ❧ *"wear out the holy ones of the Most High";* and

> ❧ *"attempt to change the sacred seasons and the law"* (v. 25).

These are the means by which human leaders were outstripping the limits of their authority and acting as divine. The short message of Daniel is that they will get what is coming to them, and that the faithful ones of the true God must endure until God delivers his unending Kingdom *"that shall never be destroyed"* (vv. 15, 27).

Power can corrupt, and absolute power can corrupt absolutely. Daniel's take on that maxim is that corrupted power is beastly. But he moves from a <u>prose</u> description of beastly rulers (vv. 2-8) to <u>poetry</u> when describing the *"Ancient One"* or *"Most High"* God (vv. 9-18). Leaders are given limited dominion to exercise authority and make decisions. But woe to any in the realm of creation who mistakes their rule for the unlimited rule of the Most High God, the only One in the realm of the Uncreated.

John P. Chandler 257

DANIEL 8

ANGELIC LEADERSHIP

*"When I, Daniel, had seen the vision, I tried to understand it.
Then someone appeared before me ... calling, "Gabriel, help
this man understand the vision." – Daniel 8:15-16*

Praying the Prophets

From the sixth to first centuries before Christ, international events had become so hostile to the Jewish people that they could only interpret these events apocalyptically. Through use of symbols, writing such as Daniel 8 makes sense of history when God's presence seems remote. In this apocalyptic vein, Daniel describes an encounter with Gabriel, the first angel identified by name in the Old Testament. In fact, only Gabriel (named here and in 9:21) and Michael (Daniel 10:13, 21, 12:1) are mentioned as angelic intermediaries. They are sent to communicate a message of hope during a confusing time from God to Daniel and to his hearers and readers.

In the Bible, whenever the angel Gabriel is mentioned, he serves as a messenger. Whenever Michael is mentioned, he serves as a guardian or warrior for God's people. The rare mention of angels occurs during a time when the close presence of God seems to have receded in the experience of God's people. The angels themselves are not the big deal; their function as a reminder that God guides history, remembers and sees his people, and will finally and decisively intervene in history is the big deal.

Leaders are not angels, but can take cues from the functions of angels in the book of Daniel. First, it's not about us. Next, we come to make things clear, not mysterious. People are often frightened and confused, and we are to bring words of hope, sustenance, and interpretation. And finally, we do not act simply out of our own identity, but on behalf of One much greater than us, One who has sent us to demonstrate assurance of divine presence and guidance of all of life. In that light, may angelic leadership abound!

John P. Chandler

DANIEL 9

REPURPOSING WISDOM

"Lord, let your face shine upon your desolated sanctuary. Incline your ear, O my God, and hear. We do not present our supplication before you on the ground of our righteousness, but on the ground of your great mercies. O Lord, hear; O Lord, forgive; O Lord, listen and act and do not delay! For your own sake, O my God, because your city and your people bear your name!" – **Daniel 9:17-19**

Praying the Prophets

Looking back over empires rising and falling, seeing Israel persecuted to the point of pogrom (v. 13), the prophet Daniel is driven to prayer. His prayer is mostly a classic petition to God for help, but he is not above turning the prayer into a sermon for third-person parties to overhear; in vv. 9-14, he talks about God rather than to God.

This is one of fifty such extended prayers in the Old Testament. Eighty-five per cent of the chapter consists of quoting or alluding to other passages in the Bible. There are echoes of the golden calf from Exodus 32 (v. 12), Aaron's benediction in Numbers 6 (v. 17) and a host of other remembrances. Daniel uses these to enrich his prayer. They call to mind the tapestry of history, a fuller picture of the prayers of God's distressed people.

Say what you will about plagiarism in a cut-and-paste age, and there is certainly a scourge of dishonesty in pretending that your thoughts owe no debt to no one else. But having said that, originality can be overrated and thin. As a leader, use all of the wisdom you can muster, but better still, use all of the wisdom you can remember, borrow, and repurpose!

Exercise: *What piece of wisdom that you have borrowed from someone else would serve you well in the decisions you face today?*

DANIEL 11

RESISTING BLASPHEMY

"He shall seduce with intrigue those who violate the covenant; but the people who are loyal to their God shall stand firm and take action." **– Daniel 11:32**

Much of the book of Daniel is *vaticinium post eventum*, a common literary feature of ancient and apocalyptic literature. It is a narration of historical events which places its teller back in ancient times. It casts the unfolding of history as a prediction, thus lending heft and authority to what is written. Chapter 11 does this by "predicting" the abominable story of Antiochus, a tyrant so arrogant that he dubbed himself "Epiphanes" (The Ephipany), claiming divine honors for himself. This tyrant famously had a pig slaughtered in the Jerusalem temple, "consecrating" it to a pagan god-of-the-day.

The characteristics of this blasphemous leader read like a laundry list of horrors:

- He is "*a contemptible person on whom royal majesty had not been conferred*" (v. 21);

- He "*obtains the kingdom through intrigue*" (v. 21), "*shall act deceitfully*" and "*become strong with a small party*" (v. 22), and "*seduces*" (v. 31);

- He "*honor(s) the god of fortresses*" (v. 38), worshiping power conveniently.

Such leadership will not stand the force of God who makes history: "*for what is determined shall be done*" (v. 36). Antiochus won some battles, but God shall surely win the war.

But this doesn't mean people stand idly by and wait for God to do all of the heavy lifting of history. "*Loyal people*" of the covenant are to engage in active resistance to any tyrant whose arrogance crosses over into blasphemy. And whether it was the Maccabees who eventually revolted in Daniel's day, the confessing church resisting the Nazis, or the Underground Railroad working against slavery in the United States, this is the call to the people of God in all such times and every place.

We are never allowed to simply bemoan leaders who step beyond their station, and who in their power pillage and plunder. We are called to resist actively the blasphemy of would-be gods, because we in covenant with the God of the Bible. And our God works for righteousness and brooks no pretenders to the divine center of reality.

DANIEL 12

"Many of those who sleep in the dust of the earth shall awake, some to everlasting life, and some to shame and everlasting contempt. Those who are wise shall shine like the brightness of the sky, and those who lead many to righteousness, like the stars forever and ever."
– Daniel 12:2-3

While there have been earlier hints of the subject (Job 19:26, Isaiah 26:19, Ezekiel 37), Daniel 12 provides the first clear mention of resurrection in the Bible. It begins a trajectory which continues throughout the rest of scripture. Talk of the resurrection is central to the ministries of Jesus (thirty allusions to Daniel's themes alone in Mark 13), Paul (1 Corinthians 15), and to the final act of the Bible in Revelation 20-22.

Resurrection is central to the Bible's view of God as Redeemer. Far from a fatalistic view of history, it takes human action, good and evil, with ultimate seriousness. Those who *"lead"* are singled out for special mention within history. Leaders, in the end, *"shine like stars."* Their luminosity is made more noteworthy in contrast to the darkness of their context.

Leaders who remember resurrection know that their own actions matter. But so do God's. And God can and will finally do what humans cannot: bring about the finally reckoning of life and history. In the midst of what seem like intractable situations, human leaders can soldier on to resuscitate, confident that only God can – and will! – raise the dead. It is the knowledge of the final victory of God that gives us hope.

"Happy are those who persevere" (v. 13), like Daniel. We can simultaneously work hard but also *"rest,"* secure in the knowledge that the God of resurrection will bring *"reward at the end of the days."* There will be a final reckoning of accounts. Thanks be to God!

HOSEA 1-3

REDEEMING FALSE LOVES

*"For I will remove the names of the Baals from her mouth,
and they shall be mentioned by name no more. I will make
for you a covenant on that day ...."* **– Hosea 2:17-18**

Hosea is the first of twelve "Minor Prophets," so named because of the relative brevity of their words. Unlike his peer, Amos, who thundered at the complacent wealthy, Hosea addressed his people who were in virtual anarchy.

Hosea's core message is one of a divine love which will not let his people go, despite their fickleness. Dramatically, Hosea enacts this message as a cuckold who has married a promiscuous woman. He names her (not his) children symbolically to demonstrate the price of the broken marriage promises. Commentator James Limburg says the names are the equivalent of naming a child today "Auschwitz" or "Hiroshima." It is a poignant picture of the huge costs of false loves.

The wayward wife has gotten into her fix because of false loves. 3:1 describers her as *"an adulteress"* who loves:

- *"other gods"* – she likes to keep her options open; and
- *"raisin cakes"* – the food of pagan festivals; she likes to party all the time.

The craving for unlimited options and constant happiness has led her to enslavement, brokenness, and despair. It always does.

Against these false loves, though, Hosea says that God will answer with covenant relationship, restoration of the marriage, fidelity to his promises, and true love. The chastisement and ruin that comes from false loves will not have the last word; God's persistent and diligent promise of faithfulness is the only thing that can overcome the costs of these false loves.

Leaders help their people understand that "love" in and of itself is not an unqualified good. To paraphrase Aristotle, one must love "the right person and to the right degree and at the right time and for the right purpose, and in the right way." All loves are not equal, and a good leader guides us toward the best kind of love that gives rather than destroying life.

John P. Chandler   269

HOSEA 4

"I will not punish your daughters when they play the whore, nor your daughters-in-law when they commit adultery; for the men themselves go aside with whores, and sacrifice with temple prostitutes; thus a people without understanding comes to ruin." – Hosea 4:14

Praying the Prophets

Like a lawyer, Hosea explains the anarchy of Exile. It has come because of:

> ➢ Bad <u>theology</u> ("*there is no knowledge of God in the land*," v. 2) has led to

> ➢ bad <u>sociology</u> ("*swearing, lying, and murder, stealing and adultery break out*," v. 3, a laundry list of broken Ten Commandments), which has led to

> ➢ bad <u>ecology</u> ("*Therefore the land mourns and all who live in it languish*," v. 4).

Because of bad theology, sociology, and ecology, creation itself is *"perishing"* (v. 3). Who is to blame? The priests. Clearly, the leaders of the people are instead *"feed on the sin of my people; they are greedy for their iniquity"* (v. 8). Somehow, the priests have an economic interest in a system that is actually destroying the land. How could this be? Hosea claims that bad leaders are involved in bad sex and bad money. Specifically, there is a system of trafficking *"daughters"* and *"daughters-in-law"* in temple prostitution. These are not promiscuous women; they are the least-free people (young, poor, and female) in a patriarchal society. Greek historian Herodotus refers to "the foulest Babylonian custom" of requiring women to, at some point in their lives, "go to the shrine of Aphrodite and there stand in line until some stranger cast money at her and then took her aside for intercourse" (cited in Beeby, p. 56). These women are not horny; they are exploited. They're not guilty; they're used. And Israel, who should know better, has bought in! Who is to blame for this state? It's convenient to blame the victim, the women involved. But Hosea instead points the finger at two other parties:

- ❧ "the men themselves (who) go aside with whores and sacrifice with temple prostitutes" (v. 14) – it is a <u>demand</u> problem at the core; it's the men who crave sex with (bought) strangers; and

- ❧ The priests who "feed on the sin of my people" and "are greedy for their iniquity" (v. 8) – leaders who are in position to do something about this old form of human trafficking and instead actually profit from the practice in some way.

This was an abomination to God then and it is one now. Prostitution is not romantic Julia Roberts in "Pretty Woman"; it is socially sanctioned rape and the destruction of young people. Every prophet or spiritual leader today is to call out bad sex tied to bad money. To turn a blind eye or silent lip in the face of it will not only get you in trouble with Hosea. You'll have to answer to God.

HOSEA 5

"Their deeds do not permit them to return to their God. For the spirit of whoredom is within them, and they do not know the Lord ... With their flocks and herds they shall go to seek the Lord, but they will not find him; he has withdrawn from them." **– Hosea 5:4, 6**

Praying the Prophets

These are shocking statements about God having *"withdrawn"* from people. If God is omnipresent, how can he choose <u>not</u> to be present with someone?

Hosea's answer, in highly sexual imagery, is that God withdraws when there are other lovers in the bedroom. *"Israel-Ephraim-Judah"* (v. 5) has *"the spirit of whoredom within them."* They love lots of gods. National gods, war gods, victory gods, fertility gods, come one, come all! Like Marilyn Monroe said, they "believe in everything, a little bit." Religion for them is like a salad bar where you can pick what you like and leave off what you don't.

One can do that – except that biblical faith does not jibe with this view of user-friendly, build-your-own-sundae religion. Hosea's prophetic faith is an exclusive, intimate, covenant partnership between God and his people. God *"knows"* (v. 3) his partner, like a lover. But a lover who comes into the chamber to find others with the covenant partner won't just happily join in. That lover will *withdraw.* At that point, you can placate with offerings (*"with their flocks and herds they shall go"*), you can take the initiative to apologize (they *"seek the Lord"*), but it ain't happening. Big love is not poly-amorous; big love is exclusive and covenantal.

The outcome is that people are left to their own bad religion. And Hosea would ask of a nation in anarchy, "How's that working out for you these days?" Those multiple royal gods to whom the people of God mistakenly turned? *"He is not able to cure you or heal your wound"* (v. 13). You don't go to a butcher when you needed a surgeon. Bad religion will *"devour"* (v. 7) its pious practitioners. You don't fix your marital problems by turning to other partners. And you don't make things right with God by being "more religious" by going after many/other gods.

Leaders help people with character decisions like perseverance over fickleness, faithfulness over wandering, fidelity over infinite choice, steadfastness over running after sirens.

HOSEA 6

MORE THAN A SONG

"For I desire steadfast love and not sacrifice, the knowledge of God rather than burnt offerings." – Hosea 6:6

God has promised his withdrawal, leaving people to their own devices. "Good luck with praying to your local gods," God is saying. "I will give you exactly what you ask for." (This is one definition of hell.) Unless and until God's people return – "*acknowledge their guilt and seek my face*," and "*beg my favor*" – God will absent himself from the situation. We get the god/God we ask for.

The response of the people to this threat of God's withdrawal from the relationship is to sing. Hosea 6:1-3 is a song of penitence. Like pilgrims going to a festival or revival and anticipating that God will automatically be moved to return, the people that they are as sure as "*rain*" that God will be back in two or three days. They believe Father God is as mechanically bound to return upon their singing as Mother Nature sends spring after winter.

But God doesn't happily prance back just because the people sing a ditty. (Especially a tune written to Mother Nature!) God doesn't say, "I will come"; he says, "You're killing me." God compares the love of the people to the morning "*dew*" (v. 4). This fleeting form of emotional response is no basis for covenant partnership. What God yearns for is loving partnership marked by steadiness, loyalty, and constancy. God aims for true love much deeper than an emotional poem or romantic song.

People want quick turnarounds, instant fixes, and songs that solve big problems. But Hosea, like every biblical prophet, and like every good leader today, knows that big solutions will take more than a song or slogan. "*Knowledge of God*" is not gained through emotional rituals but through "*steadfast love*." And when love is steadfast, constant, long-term, and beyond the winds of emotion, the God of the Bible can do great things with and through his partners.

John P. Chandler   277

HOSEA 7

HALF-BAKED AND

BIRD-BRAINED

"Ephraim is a cake not turned ... Ephraim has become like a dove, silly and without sense; they call upon Egypt, they go to Assyria." – Hosea 7:8, 11

Praying the Prophets

Hosea 7 is brackets laments from God (vv. 1f, 13ff – yes, God takes our straying personally and is emotionally upset) around indictments of what has gotten Israel in such a mess. The culprit is bad leadership, especially regarding king-making and foreign policy. Recalling a series of assassinations after the reign of Jeroboam, Hosea describes a nation that has rejected its identity as God's chosen people, delivered miraculously from Egypt. Instead, they favor conspiracy, compromise, and conniving.

Specifically, Hosea describes the bad (political) leadership of the day using two images:

- ❧ Israel is a "bad baker" (vv. 4-8) – like an over-heated oven (vv. 4, 6) or slothful attendant who forgets to turn the cake so that it is raw on one side and burnt on the other. The sins here are intemperate rage ("*their heart burns within them*," v. 6) and careless neglect.

- ❧ Israel is a stupid bird, "*a dove silly and without sense*" (vv. 11-12) – foolishly leaving the safety of the (divine) nest, straying into the teeth of danger ("*Egypt, Assyria*"), thinking they are sources of help when they are in fact predators.

The fundamental sins are short-sightedness and naive stupidity. Israel's bad leaders are half-baked and bird-brained!

As always in leadership, the core problems are theological. In conniving king-making and short-sighted straying, Israel has rejected her fundamental identity as a representative of a unique relationship with God for the rest of the world to see. A strong biblical leader, political or otherwise, never forgets their core identity as covenant partner with the God of the Bible. This is the final safeguard against half-baked and bird-brained leadership.

John P. Chandler 279

HOSEA 8

KING-MAKING AND ALTAR-BREAKING

"They made kings, but not through me; they set up princes, but without my knowledge. With their silver and gold they made idols for their own destruction." **– Hosea 8:4**

Like a *"trumpet"* (v. 1), Hosea sounds an alarm for impending destruction. Israel has sown the wind and is about to *"reap the whirlwind"* (v. 7) and *"return to Egypt"* (v. 13, always a symbol for bondage).

Why the doom? Two principal reasons:

1. Improper king-making – *"They made kings but not through me"*; and

2. Unholy ways of dealing with forgiveness – *"When Ephraim multiplied altars to expiate sin, they became to him altars for sinning"* (v. 11).

To the prophet, the spheres of national wrongdoing were first political, and second moral or justice-related. When leaders are improperly elevated, and when sin or crime is not properly dealt with, a nation will *"reap the whirlwind."*

In modern parlance, leaders must not be placed according to the highest bidder, and pardon cannot be cheap. When one is *"made king"* or *"prince"* in unholy ways, people get the bad king they deserve. And when someone can go to any local altar and be forgiven too quickly and easily for serious wrong-doing with a casual wave of the hand, then a community will experience a *"fire"* that *"devours"* (v. 14). A righteous community takes election and justice with holy seriousness.

John P. Chandler   281

HOSEA 9–10

SPEED, BUILDING, GROWTH?

"Israel is a luxuriant vine that yields its fruit. The more his fruit increased the more altars he built; as his country improved, he improved his pillars. Their heart is false; now they must bear their guilt." – Hosea 10:1-2

Sometimes the prophet is a party-pooper, and when Hosea shows up as God's *"sentinel"* (9:8) at the feast of Succoth to tell revelers that trouble is on the way, Israel cries, *"The prophet is a fool, the man of the spirit is mad!"* (9:7). Yeah, kill the messenger.

Hosea's indictment is that Israel has mutated a festival thanking God for provision into a pagan fertility celebration. It is still plenty "religious," but is a prostituting of their faith and national calling. Such has corrupted the people, who *"became detestable like the thing they loved"* (9:10). We always become like what we worship.

All of this trouble hatched in a prosperous time when Israel's *"fruit increased"* (11:1). Because of ease and surplus, leaders engineered construction of more altars – which multiplied the pagan rites. For the first time in the Bible, it is Israel's priests (not pagans) who are dubbed *"idolatrous"* (10:5). And national leaders are no better; they *"have trust in (their) power and in the multitude of warriors"* (v. 13). They are in for a fall.

One would think that national prosperity, thriving religious culture, and a strong military are a recipe for Israel's success. But they are not, when these things simply lead a nation to run faster in the wrong direction. Speed, building, and growth? These are not unqualified goods. Cancer can grow quickly, too!

Leaders do well to use the right metrics, and those are never simply matters of speed, building, and growth. They are matters of *"righteousness"* and *"steadfast love"* (10:12), matters that are on the heart of God.

Exercise: *Are "speed, building, and growth" your metrics for success in leadership? Meditate on whether this is so, if it is okay, and what you want to do about it.*

HOSEA 11

"...for I am a God and no mortal, the Holy One in your midst, and I will not come in wrath." – **Hosea 11:9**

Chapter 11 is not only the center-point of the book of Hosea, but, in the opinion of many, the heart of the Old Testament and its clearest statement of the divine heart for the people of God. Along with the Isaiah 53 picture of the suffering servant, Hosea 11's portrayal of God's transcendence-yet-condescension-to-care prefigures the incarnation of Jesus as the fullest and final expression of who God is and how God deals with the human creation.

At some point, every human symbol portraying God's love for us breaks down. We can use the finest expressions of human love – marriage, parental love, friendship – but at some point they are inadequate metaphors. Beyond all human logic which demands consistency is God's way of working with us. In the divine logic, at the end of the day, God's "heart recoils within," and "compassion grows warm and tender," and God withholds from executing his justified "fierce anger" (vv. 8f). Though logically God has every right to lay into a "people ... bent on turning away" (v. 7), God chooses instead, again and again, to love:

> "Yet it was I who taught Ephraim to walk, I took them up in my arms; but they did not know that I healed them. I led them with cords of human kindness, with bands of love. I was to them like those who lift infants to their cheeks. I bent down to them and fed them." – Hosea 11:3-4

God relinquishes his rights to be angry. God transcends the logic of consistency and instead imposes a final logic of compassion.

A leader can always fuss at his or her people. There is forever a logical reason to do so, and people are forever doing things that deserve the chastisement of the leader. But those who would lead in the way of the God of Hosea 11 will, at the end of the day, value compassion over symmetry, restoration over punishment, warmth over reason, and love over logic.

John P. Chandler

HOSEA 12

PICK A BETTER LEADER

"The Lord has an indictment against Judah and will punish Jacob according to his ways, and repay him according to his deeds ... But for you, return to your God, hold fast to love and justice, and wait continually for your God."
– Hosea 12:2, 6

Hosea's diagnosis of what ails and can cure his people (Judah) lies in his comparison of Judah with their archetypal ancestor, Jacob. The nut (Judah) didn't fall far from the tree (Jacob). And herein lay the problem: Judah has chosen the wrong hero and is now imitating Jacob in all the wrong ways.

Jacob, though a traditional hero, is pictured in Hosea 12 through three ugly snapshots: grabbing his twin's first-born status (v. 3), arrogantly daring to wrestle with the angel of God himself (v. 4), and bragging about his cunning gain of wealth at the expense of others (v. 7). Jacob's story is one of cheating, selfishness, and cruelty. And now Judah fancies itself as successor to this heritage: "Ephraim has said, *"Ah, I am rich, I have gained wealth for myself; in all of my gain no offense has been found in me that would be sin"* (v. 8; the same words repeated by the church of Laodicea in Revelation 3:17).

But Hosea tells them that have chosen the wrong hero and need to pick a better story. He tells them of Moses and his successors, the prophets (v. 13), suggesting that this story of liberation is the way to *"return to your God and hold fast to love and justice."*

There is no problem with identifying heroes. We all do it, and these heroes we pick can be a key lens through which we establish our identity and vocation. But woe to the person, group, or nation who picks the wrong hero and the stories that go with that hero. Like Hosea, a leader has to call out those who are emulating the wrong heroes. We can choose any number of stories about our heritage, character, and future. The stories and heroes we choose shape us. So leaders demand that people pick the best stories. We are called to pick a better hero.

Prayer*: At the end of the day, O God, help me today to choose Jesus Christ as my hero, the one whose stories become my own. I reject all other false and small stories for myself. And I ask that my life follow in the trajectory of the life of this One who came to serve and give his life for many. So I pray in his name, Amen.*

HOSEA 13

GREAT GIFTS, GREAT EXPECTATIONS

"People are kissing calves! Therefore they shall be like the morning mist or like the dew that goes away early, like chaff that swirls from the threshing floor, or like smoke from a window." – Hosea 13:2-3

Hosea 13 is a fearsome, trembling word. In v. 9, the prophet asks precisely the opposite of Paul's question in Romans 8:31; Hosea says (speaking for God), "*I will destroy you, O Israel; who can help you?*" If God is against you, who could possibly help or save you? A fearsome thing to contemplate, indeed.

How and why have the people of God gotten into such a state? The primary reason is that they have been given great gifts and unique opportunities - and they have squandered them.

- ☞ God gave his people "*silver*" – and they fashioned idols out of it (vv. 2-3);

- ☞ God gave his people election and "*fed you in the wilderness*," providing Promised Land –and the people "*were satisfied, and their heart was proud*" (vv. 4-6); and

- ☞ God answered the prayers of the people and gave them kings – and the people turned their trust to a human king rather than God as their King (vv. 10f).

Hosea is unsparing in his declaration of God's judgment. When you have gifts of silver, of divine provision, of great leadership – and **then** you squander them – great will be your fall, and the judgment of God will be devastating.

He gives four images of what happens to leaders who fumble. They become "*morning mist, dew that goes away early, chaff that swirls from the threshing floor, or like smoke from a window.*" Poof, gone. Jesus would later echo Hosea 13 in Mark 4:25: "*For to those who have, more will be given; and from those who have nothing, even what they have will be taken away.*"

Leaders must understand that with gifts and opportunity come corresponding expectation. Hosea 13 says to us, "Sober up! God has given you much, and the bigger you are, the harder you can fall." We need not spend all of our reflection asking whether God is being fair in this; better is that we take a look in the mirror and get moving. A good leader will not be immobilized but activated by such a prophetic warning.

John P. Chandler   289

HOSEA 14

"O Ephraim, what have I to do with idols? It is I who answer and look after you. I am like an evergreen cypress; your faithfulness comes from me." – **Hosea 14:8**

Every book of the Bible gives voice to the great news of God's love and salvation for his people. Genesis says that the work of God is to move us from darkness to light; Exodus, from bondage to liberation; the Gospels, from death to resurrection. And Hosea says that the wonder of God is that, when, like an unfaithful marriage partner, we had willfully strayed from vows of faithfulness to our covenant partner God, there is yet hope for the future. The adultery may be deadly, but it is not the fatal, final word.

There is hope because of the constancy of God, who describes himself as "*like an evergreen cypress.*" Like a tree that does not drop its leaves in the wind, nor lose its color in the winter, nor change with the seasons ... so is the nature of God whose "*faithfulness*" to his promises to us (thankfully) does not depend on our whims and fickleness. It is the great expression of hope for the world in the Bible: that in the end, God's goodness is greater than all of our badness.

The first thing a leader should do in reflecting on this is to pause and give thanks! We are nowhere near infallible as leaders; and yet, God's care for us does not, mercifully, depend on our leadership performance. Leaders embrace the divine grace extended to them, which leads to a humility and gratitude necessary for what Jim Collins calls, "level-five leadership."

Second, wise leaders will note the constancy of God, the unalterable divine will to love us (often despite ourselves). It is this faithfulness, this unchanging commitment that can transform a fickle lover. Great leaders understand that market conditions change, employees wax and wane, business evolves, and culture never stands still. But the final work of leadership is not to surf the ever-changing environment around us. It is, rather, to remain planted and clear about who we are, Whose we are, and what we are here to do. With that constancy that comes from God's constancy as the core of who we are, we are able to lead with calm clarity in great works of restoration.

John P. Chandler

JOEL 2

"Yet even now, says the Lord, return to me with all your
heart, with fasting, with weeping, and with mourning; rend
your hearts and not your clothing. Return to the Lord, your
God, for he is gracious and merciful, slow to anger, and
abounding in steadfast love, and relents from punishing."
– Joel 2:12-13

The brief words of Joel interpret a national crisis, a devastating locust plague. The book lacks historical references because it intends to model how leaders timelessly respond to calamity. Joel demonstrates how a leader can and must interpret tragedy, challenge people to respond appropriately, and offer words of genuine hope. How does a leader do this? With:

1. Unblinking Honesty. First, Joel laments and names the terror. Things are awful! Denying the facts is useless and dishonest.

2. Intentional Empowerment. Then, rather than assuming that people are helpless, Joel calls them to do what they can in a crisis. He empowers people to act. Specifically, people are to "call a solemn assembly" (1:14). They are to "gather" and particularly to "fast" – this is a time to do without some of the comforts that can insulate us from the reality of horror and prevent us from devoting our full attention to asking God for help. We are not paralyzed; we can and must "gather" with each other in order to "return" to God with our hearts.

3. Unapologetic Hopefulness. Finally, rather than shrinking back from speaking about God's hand in the crisis, Joel moves toward it. He declares that the plague is no random occurrence, something a sniveling, helpless God wished to prevent but could not. It is not, and actually portends an even more massive upheaval: the "Day of the Lord" (2:31), God's final judgment. If you think locusts are bad, wait until the very sun and moon disappear!

John P. Chandler   293

Though this final word seems ominous, Joel in the end frames and interprets crisis through the lens of hope. He speaks bluntly to the anguish. But beyond mere description of pain, Joel leads by declaring that while the calamity is great, it is not greater than the God who is Lord of all, including Lord of the future. History is not random and tragedy is not meaningless. Even devastation can be used for the betterment of all things when, because of it, people (re) discover that "*the heavens and the earth shake, but the Lord is a refuge for his people, a stronghold ...*" (3:16).

Leaders step up and into the crucible of crisis. They do their irreplaceable work with speech that is unblinkingly honest, communally empowering, and unapologetically hopeful.

Exercise: *Given what you are facing as a decision-maker, what would be more helpful right now – fasting, or gathering? Do you need to do without some normal necessities to reboot your mind and heart, or do you need to embed yourself within the community of faith in a way that turns you toward God's clarity? Both are part of the rhythm of leadership. Ask God for which is called for in your next measure.*

Praying the Prophets

AMOS 2

"Thus says the Lord: For three transgressions of Moab, and for four, I will not revoke the punishment; because he burned to lime the bones of the king of Edom. So I will send a fire on Moab ..." – Amos 2:1-2

During a long, peaceful, prosperous reign in eighth century B.C. Israel, a plain-spoken, small-town lay person with a southern accent came north. He walked to the microphone speaking harsh words in a smooth season. The prophet Amos denounced any who would smugly rely on a prosperity and military might which insulates them from a sense of accountability to God or neighbor.

In chapters 1-2, Amos begins his broadside against traditional enemies (Syria and the Philistines), moves to include kin rivals (Tyre, Ammon, Moab, Edom), and denounces archrival Judah. Then he turns the mirror on Israel and scathingly declares the judgment of God on people who thought they had special privileges. Israel's laundry-list of abuses is longer, and her punishments will be more severe – because Israel has a history with God and should, of all nations, know better.

One of the abuses for which people will be held accountable is seen in Amos' striking line about the "*transgressions of Moab*." Namely, Moab "*burned to lime the bones*" of their enemies. This lime was then used to make plaster and whitewash – consumer products – to decorate the lavish homes of the oppressors. Amos says the fire they used to manufacture this is nothing when compared to the fire that God will send on anyone who does this to the powerless.

When does a leader roar? A leader roars when the abused are voiceless. A leader calls down fire from heaven when the powerful burn other human beings into consumable products. A person is never, ever, to be a commodity trafficked for the luxury of the rich. Whenever they are, God roars – and a good leader or prophet is a tool in the hand of the Almighty to roar as well.

AMOS 3

NO SECRETS
TO LEADERSHIP

*"Surely the Lord God does nothing without revealing his
secret to his servants the prophets." – Amos 3:7*

Special opportunity requires corresponding accountability. Amos saves his harshest denunciations for the people of Israel who have been given the best chance to represent the interests of God in and to the world, and even then fail.

In light of Israel's failure to lead in the world, Amos fires off a series of rhetorical questions in vv. 3-8, including:

- ❧ "Does a lion roar in the forest when it has no prey?

- ❧ Does a bird fall into a snare on the earth when there is no trap?

- ❧ Is a trumpet blown in a city (to herald war) and the people are not afraid?"

The purpose of these rapid-fire questions is to elicit quick, unanimous responses: Yes, of course. It is obvious. Amos gets his audience to say yes, yes, yes – and then delivers the coup: "Surely the Lord God does nothing without revealing his secret to his servants the prophets." It is not that God is trying to keep his will as a hidden secret, available to only to a few. What God wants is clear, obvious … and undone.

The earliest heresy in Christianity was Gnosticism, the idea that special revelation was available only to a few. If you didn't have insider knowledge (gnosis), well, it stinks to be you. This has never been true in the Bible. What God wants from people is obvious. And God's people have not failed because they did not know any better. They failed because they did not do what they knew to do. When there is no execution … there is execution!

Contrary to common teaching today, there are no leadership "secrets." A good leader will make it very clear what it is s/he expects people to do. And a good leader will never let us be educated beyond the level of our obedience.

Exercise: *Name the clear and obvious thing that God wants you to do next. Without subtleties, without clauses, state it in a simple sentence. Write it down if that helps. And then make it your motto until you hear the next clear thing God wants you to do.*

AMOS 4

UNPOPULAR, WELL-PLACED ACCOUNTABILITY

"Hear this word, you cows of Bashan ... who oppress the poor, who crush the needy, who say to their husbands, "Bring something to drink!" The Lord has sworn by his holiness: The time is surely coming upon you, when they take you away with hooks, even the last of you with fishhooks."
– Amos 4:1-2

As only a plain-spoken country person speaking to urban sophisticates can do, Amos in chapter 4 lambasts the religious women of Israel. He starts by calling them "cows." So much for *"How to Win Friends and Influence People!"*

Amos decries these women who "oppress the poor" and "crush the needy." How so? Through the constant demand that their husbands, *"Bring something to drink."* They have a certain lifestyle and insist on maintaining already-attained watermarks of comfort and affluence – even as those same demands destroy survival margins for "the least of these" in society.

Furthermore, these fat *"cows"* are very devout, church-going people, going to altars at Bethel and Gilgal (v. 4). Amos says, worship away – *"and multiply transgression."* Church attendance, tithing, and piety when unaccompanied by adjustments in how you treat your neighbors only make things worse, as Jesus (Matthew 23) and James (1:26f) would later echo. The outcome? Amos says these overfed, self-indulgent secondary oppressors will be led away with harpoons (*"fishhooks,"* v. 2). And soon enough, so they were.

Beyond his frank bluntness, a leader may take note of Amos' diagnostic acumen. He does not go after the easy targets of national downfall (bad kings) but the root source: fat, demanding *"cows."* Consumer demand and greed form the heart of the problem, and Amos is unafraid to hold accountable those who feed demand. In our day, it is easy to blame drug cartels in Columbia or human trafficking rings in India for societal problems, and they are true contributors. But unless and until we hold a mirror to ordinary people in the U.S. who insist on buying sex and drugs – to consumer demand – we are passing the buck.

Prophetic leadership in unafraid to do the unpopular work of well-placed accountability.

John P. Chandler   303

AMOS 5

MOVE IT OUTDOORS!

"*I hate, I despise your festivals ... But let justice roll down like waters, and righteousness like an ever-flowing stream.*"
— **Amos 5:21, 24**

Amos' most well-known words cannot be reduced to a shopworn cliché critiquing ritual. He is more pointedly speaking about the proper location of our responsiveness to God, our Leader.

"*Hate*" and "*despise*" are strong words, but God's rejection of indoor piety lounging comfortably alongside of outdoor social injustice is comprehensive. Such descriptions allude to the opposite of a burnt sacrifice which is supposed to leave a pleasing aroma in the nostrils of God. Instead, Amos says that it all stinks to high heaven: "*festivals, assemblies, offerings, songs*" (vv. 21f). Why? Because simultaneously in the public square, the city "*gates*" and "*streets*" (v. 15), there is no justice for the widow, orphan, or immigrant.

Justice for Amos is not a western picture of a blind woman holding scales in a balance. It is a mighty, rolling, and "*ever-flowing stream.*" It is dynamic and aggressive, not conceptual or theoretical. Justice is not static, but moves and removes. It is not blind but visionary. And herein lay the problem for the prophet. When the people of God expend all of their movement inside their solemn assemblies while remaining unmoved by the plight of those outside in the city gates, God thinks that this stinks. If justice is a mighty stream, then a river is for outdoors.

Good leaders don't let those they lead do all of their "moving" inside the house. They don't allow the best energies of people to be expended on internal matters. Rather, they push people outside, where they cleanse corrupt streets and actively advocate for the weak. The real work of devotion is not only in the sanctuary but also in the streets. Move it outdoors, insists the prophet. What God wants are not quiet scales but mighty streams of justice!

AMOS 6

"Alas for those who are at east in Zion, and for those who feel secure on Mount Samaria, the notables of the first of the nations, to whom the house of Israel resorts!"
– Amos 6:1

Amos 6 is not directed at the general population but specifically targets leaders. More precisely, the prophet has something to say to those who are privileged and who enjoy the perks that come with leadership. The military today says, "R.H.I.P. – Rank has its Privileges." Amos warns the highly ranked of what follows the abuses of those privileges.

Seven verbs of ease describe the life of leaders whose personal affluence is mixed in a deadly cocktail with social indifference: these privileged leaders *"lie on beds, lounge on their couches, eat lambs/calves, sing idle songs, improvise, drink wine from bowls (not goblets), anoint themselves with the finest oils"* (vv. 4-6). These are verbs of leisure, not leadership. The behaviors lie exclusively in the domain of the *"first"* in society, and Amos says they will result in another *"first"*: *"Therefore they shall now be the first to go into exile, and the revelry of the loungers shall pass away"* (v. 7).

It is often not the crucible of external conflict and challenge but the slow inner erosion of character that presents the most deadly danger to leaders. A steady diet of ease, security, and privilege can seduce and weaken a leader to the point where s/he no longer has the fortitude to lead from personal, inner character, and must instead *"resort"* to find strength from *"the notables of the first of other nations."* And if you dine with the devil, you better have a long spoon!

Yes, rank has its privileges. But privilege has its unique dangers. And the leader who ignores the seduction of perks will be the first and worst to fall.

Exercise: *Is there any particular privilege of my leadership that is putting me spiritually at-risk today? Ask God for a high sense of alertness so that this privilege doesn't cause me (or anyone else) to stumble.*

John P. Chandler

AMOS 7

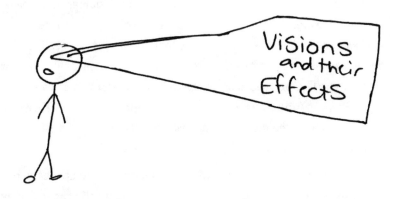

"Then Amos answered Amaziah, "I am no prophet, nor
a prophet's son; but I am a herdsman, and a dresser of
sycamore trees, and the Lord took me from following the
flock, and The Lord said to me, 'Go, prophesy to my people
Israel.' Now therefore hear the word of the Lord ..."
– Amos 7:14-16

Like many, but not all, prophets and leaders, Amos is given powerful vision. Chapter 7 is a series of dreams surrounding the prophet's famous confrontation with the official national priest, Amaziah, who just wants Amos to go away (vv. 12f). Four dreams – God judging as a plague of *"locusts"* (v. 1), *"shower of fire"* (v. 4), *"plumb line"* determining irreparable warping (vv. 7ff), and an almost-rotten *"basket of summer fruit"* (8:1f) – are powerful. But the four visions/dreams in and of themselves are not important. What is important is what these dreams put into effect.

These God-given visions envelop Amos' famous confrontation with the state-sponsored priest, Amaziah. Official Amaziah is a bought man, sent to bless whatever the king Jeroboam wants and to declare it as the word of the Lord. (State-sponsored priests are a terrible idea!) Amaziah says nothing about the content of Amos' devastating judgment on the nation; he simply asks Amos to go back home and say what he has to say there, not here *"in the king's sanctuary"* (v. 13 – who is being worshiped in this sanctuary anyway?). But Amos has come to speak the hard word of God, and does not shrink away from declaring his visions when and where God tells him to say them. The brutal fate of Amaziah to come is only a foreshadowing of a much-larger national disaster.

Simply having a dream doesn't make one a leader. A leader is someone who takes God-dreams and turns them into reality. All of the visions of Amos would amount to nothing had he not chosen to speak truth to power by confronting the court prophet, king, and nation is such a risky way. Dreams, though eloquent and inspiring, are tools for leaders only when measured by their social outcomes. Vision is useful only when it has communal effects.

John P. Chandler   309

AMOS 8

"We will make the ephah small and the shekel great, and practice deceit with false balances, buying the poor for silver and the needy for a pair of sandals, and selling the sweepings of the wheat." **– Amos 8:6**

Amos' fearlessness as a leader is all-encompassing. He has taken on society women (4:1ff), the professional guild of religious leaders (7:10ff), neighboring nations (friend and enemy, chapters 1-2), and political leaders, including kings. Like the honey badger, he don't care. He is not a bought leader; he values the opinions of God more than the interests of any powers-that-be.

Into this larger context, Amos in chapter 8 unmasks the greed of the merchant community in his day. Their Better Business Bureau is outwardly scrupulous, closing shop on holy days. But they regard such closings with disdain, impatiently muttering that all this religious nonsense is bad for business. They want to open on the Sabbath and get back to the more-important focus on making money.

And once open for business, the merchants defraud in three ways. They:

1. *"make the ephah small"* – Instead of a full bushel, customers are deceived into receiving slightly less than they paid for;

2. *"practice deceit with false balances"* by making *"the shekel great"* – they rig the scales with inaccurate weights, again cheating customers; and

3. are *"selling the sweepings of the wheat"* – they pass off scrap as genuine; not until later do buyers realize they have unknowingly purchased junk.

Who is hurt most by these commercial practices? Of course, it is the *"poor."* They are bought *"for silver"* and sold *"for a pair of sandals."* Amos declares that the divine day of reckoning is at hand

John P. Chandler   311

for such merchants. Indeed, they were among the first to be put out of business when God sends exile to the nation.

In our day, it is common to say, "Business is business" in an attempt to exempt mercantile practices from any call to care for the poor. "I'm not in business to save the world but to make a living." But a holy life encompasses the whole of life. And God pays attention to the shekels, scales, and silver in business, because God pays attention to the poor (and to the rich). God cares for the moral and social realms of business – and business people better care for them, too.

AMOS 9

"The Lord, God of hosts, he who touches the earth and it melts ... who builds his upper chambers in the heavens, and founds his vault upon the earth; who calls for the waters of the sea, and pours them out upon the surface of the earth – the Lord is his name." – Amos 9:5-6

Commentator James Ward asks of Amos, "*Is it possible for pride of place and attachment to place to undermine obedience to God?*" (Ward, p. 49) The short answer for the prophet to his audience was yes. The people of Israel had allowed power, place, and prosperity to go to their heads. They were invincible. They were arrogant. And they were wrong, and destroyed because of it.

In the midst of descriptions about destruction of place, Amos inserts a hymn about the nature and power of God. God, sings the prophet, is a builder. And not simply Thomas Jefferson's now-passive deist divinity, who once built the earth as a clock, then wound it up, but now has no more to do with it. God instead actively continues building in the earth. God "*melts, builds, founds, calls, pours*" (vv. 5-6). God "*repairs, raises, rebuilds*" (v. 11) – all of these are verbs of ongoing activity and divine involvement in the affairs and places of the world. This Builder creates places (v. 6) and delivers people (v. 7).

All of this is in stark contrast to a nation which would soon disappear, and for this reason it is part of Amos' grand finale. As Ward says, "*The institutions we participate in and hold dear are finite, imperfect, and subject to eventual disappearance. We should not stake our happiness or the meaning of our lives upon them.*" This is true of homes, churches, and nations. Sanctuaries and nations may fall, and speech may grow silent (8:11). But God is a Builder.

When we lead with an awareness that our allegiance to and direction is from the Builder rather than trusting in any of the things, institutions, and places we ourselves have built, then we may swim in the mighty stream of justice of prophets like Amos. And we can lead by assisting the master Builder in the creation of the beloved communities for which we were put on earth.

John P. Chandler

OBADIAH

NO INNOCENT BYSTANDERS

"On the day that you stood aside, on the day that strangers carried off his wealth, and foreigners entered his gates and cast lots for Jerusalem, you too were like one of them."
– Obadiah v. 11

The shortest book in the Old Testament blisters nearby kin who refused to help Judah when enemies attacked and plundered. Hearkening back to the story of twins Jacob (Judah) and Esau (Edom) in strife, the prophet Obadiah forcefully and bitterly reprimands the failure of a neighbor to help in a crisis. Judah is deported by conquering Babylonians. But instead of coming to the rescue, Edom joins in the "*gloating*" (vv. 8ff) of the victors. It is a massive betrayal, and the prophet promises that Edom will face a reckoning of equal proportion on "*the day of the Lord.*" "*As you have done, so it shall be done to you; your deeds shall return on your own head*" (v. 15).

The prophets believe that there is a moral symmetry and coherence to the universe. Obadiah's chief contribution to voicing this is his insistence that there is no such thing as an "*innocent bystander.*" If you see a neighbor in deep trouble and fail to help, you are morally accountable for this failure to help. You cannot, like those who preceded the Good Samaritan in Luke 10, simply "*pass by on the other side*" when you see a neighbor in distress. Where you hoped to go and what you planned to do can never take precedence over the neighbor for whom you are responsible. "*Anyone, then, who knows the right thing to do and fails to do it, commits sin*" (James 4:17).

Moral leadership involves modeling and teaching others to live with a sense of accountability for the fate of others beyond ourselves. We have not discharged the sum of our ethical duty when we simply avoid trouble/sin and take care of our own business. The world governed by God is not meant to be a place where people solely fend for themselves. We have neighbors, and the responsibility to help them in their day of distress lies squarely on our shoulders.

John P. Chandler

JONAH 1

HOLIER THAN THOU

"The captain came and said to (Jonah), "What are you doing sound asleep? Get up, call on your god! Perhaps the god will spare us a thought so that we do not perish." – Jonah 1:6

Praying the Prophets

Jonah ("dove") is a symbol for the people of God in their refusal to be a people on a mission to and for the rest of the world. It is a story in which the deity is mentioned 39 times in 44 verses. And it is characterized by how God uses "outsiders" – sailors, storms, a great fish, and the city of Nineveh – as vehicles in the hand of God to demonstrate what God hopes for in people. Jonah, on the other hand, is everything that God drives crazy: insular, petulant, stubborn, and argumentative.

The story is told in a deeply ironic (and funny) way. Jonah, the missionary, finds creative ways not to live out his faith. The supposedly irreligious sailors, on the other hand, are devout (they pray!) and are open to conversion (vv. 14, 16). The point is the contrast; who acts like the people of God and who doesn't? Who is "holier than thou?"

Regardless of one's title as a leader, it is critical that the leader live up to the name. We are in deep trouble as leaders if the people who do not share our title, position, or "official" designation of being in charge act more like leaders than we do. We are rightly viewed as hypocrites when we hold the title but do not have the character to match. Nothing could be more important for a leader than to hold the highest moral, ethical, and theological ground in the room.

JONAH 3

"When God saw what they did, how they turned from their evil ways, God changed his mind about the calamity that he had said he would bring upon them; and he did not do it."
— Jonah 3:10

Given a second chance, Jonah is called by God to go on a mission. He does so, but without gusto. Preaching to Nineveh, city of Israel's Exile, was as distasteful as a post-war Jew speaking at Dachau. His message is unadorned and blunt, without persuasive rhetoric: *"Forty days more, and Nineveh shall be overthrown!"* (v. 4).

But, to his amazement (and disgust), the king and all of the people hear the message, repent, and believe. This upsets Jonah; he wanted Nineveh to get what was coming to them, and he sulks when they are spared because they have changed. Worse still, God *"changed his mind"* or repents about Nineveh! The only character in the story unwilling to change is Jonah. This is why the story of Jonah ends not with a creedal statement but a question (4:11). It asks whether <u>we</u> are as open to change as we should be.

Any leader who wants to see change in those who follow must be simultaneously open to change within him or her-self. True persuasion requires 360-degree openness to being persuaded. We gain the moral platform and relational credibility to lead others to change when we do not place ourselves above the need to be open to being moved. Every leader must be able to say to others, "I can be had by a better idea." After all, if God is open to changing his mind, what would exempt us from the need to be open?

Exercise: *Where might I need to open myself to the possibility that someone else has a better idea that would change my mind and approach to a leadership situation? Give yourself over to that possibility today.*

John P. Chandler

MICAH 2

PREACHING DISGRACEFULLY

"Do not preach" – thus they preach – "one should not preach about such things; disgrace will overtake us."
– Micah 2:6

In Israel, land was power. If you had land, you had a financial future; if not, you were at the mercy of those around you who could do as they pleased with you. Micah, a working-class prophet in the late eighth century B.C., preaches a very unpopular message. Those in power are wrongfully seizing the land of poorer people in order to accumulate more. Micah says to them, God is watching and you will pay! Micah will not stand silently and watch those in charge make a blatant land-grab which drives women and children "out from their pleasant homes" (v. 9).

What is amazing is that other preachers denounce Micah for speaking up. "Do not preach" on such things, they say; it is disgraceful. Such is the silent complicity of spiritual "leaders" who are in fact nothing more than the arm of the powerful, justifying their greed.

But true leaders always speak out against covetousness, even if it appears socially impolite. Micah will not let those in charge destroy "my people" (v. 8), even as other preachers wish he would lower his voice and change the subject. The prophet fears God and speaks for the voiceless; his audience is not those who currently occupy seats of power.

It is never the wrong time to do the right thing. Like Micah, a leader must sometimes preach "disgracefully" – impolitely, distastefully to high society, on subjects that indict public figures. Because to covet and to oppress the voiceless are never okay. Woe to the preacher who remains silent in the face of these offenses against God and the poor.

John P. Chandler   323

MICAH 3

UNTANGLING SELF-INTEREST

"Thus says the Lord concerning the prophets who lead my people astray, who cry "Peace" when they have something to eat, but declare war against those who put nothing into their mouths. Therefore it shall be night to you, without vision, and darkness to you, without revelation …" – Micah 3:5-6

To Micah, leadership matters. He places the blame for the fall of the city squarely on the *"heads of Jacob"* and *"rulers of the house of Israel"* (v. 1). Like butchers and cannibals (v. 2), they carve up the nation because *"rulers, priests, and prophets"* have been bought with *"a bribe, a price, and for money"* (v. 11).

Micah's harshest words are for religious defenders of the rich whose theologies justify the oppression of the poor. They are nothing more than mercenary prophets and pay-per-view seers. In the words of commentator James Limburg, they put "honoraria over honor" and "fees over faith." In short, they vote only with their pocketbooks. Their personal economic interests indelibly shape and distort their solemn office. Micah forecasts their deafness to revelation and their public disgrace. He declares his own freedom to speak with power because he is not a bought man (vv. 7-8).

Financial self-interest is a powerful thing, and has the ability to cause eloquent leaders entrusted with public vision to reduce their message. Every leader must guard against being tangled in a web of self-interest. To be reduced to speaking favorably about whatever gives us something to eat is to prostitute ourselves and betray the public's trust in us. It will result in silence from God and a ruined city.

Exercise: *Is there any area of my life and leadership that may be compromised (actually or potentially) by financial self-interest? What steps might I need to take to guard against any "love of money" that could pollute how God wants me to speak and lead today?*

John P. Chandler

MICAH 4

"... they shall beat their swords into plowshares, and their spears into pruning hooks; nation shall not lift up sword against nation, neither shall they learn war any more; but they shall all sit under the own vines and under their own fig trees, and not one shall make them afraid, for the mouth of the Lord has spoken." – Micah 4:3-4

Here Micah quotes a vision identical to that of Isaiah 2:2-4. These words of disarmament are famously inscribed on the walls of the United Nations, naming their hopes. The prophet does not express the popular hopes of the people for military victory over their oppressors. Rather, he names a different dream altogether.

Micah's dreams are those of a farmer – "*vines* and *figs*" – and not dreams of conquering kings and generals. Commentator Juan Alfaro says it is impossible to dream of both simultaneously:

> "*The triumph of the Lord will be the death sentence to the arms race ... military maneuvers will be turned into sports festivals, tanks into tractors, bullets into bread, rifles into spades, missiles into fireworks, and planes into agricultural sprayers*" (Alfaro, p. 49).

Thus Micah does not simply announce the fulfillment of national hopes. Instead, he names the dream of God as something far grander than what people have been hoping for. They wanted to win wars; God wants to create time and space where such fighting was unnecessary, and all energy that once went into war was instead devoted to fruitfulness and productivity.

A leader never simply panders to what people ask for. Sometimes, it is the role of a leader to determine that the current dreams are far too small, and to alter them until they cast a holy vision that is far more expansive.

MICAH 6

THE GREAT TRIANGLE

"He has told you, O mortal, what is good; and what does the Lord require of you but to do justice, and to love kindness, and to walk humbly with your God?" – Micah 6:8

These grand words, quoted by Jimmy Carter at his presidential inauguration, summarize not only the book of Micah but the core of the Old Testament prophets. God does not want things ("*burnt offerings,*" v. 6) but wants the hearts of people. God hates victimhood (v. 7) and has a higher aspiration for humanity. God is looking for partnership with pilgrims who "*do justice, love kindness, and walk humbly.*"

In Micah's view, "*justice*" is more than law-keeping; it is advocacy for the voiceless. "*Mercy*" is more than feelings; it is vibrant communal solidarity. And "*to walk humbly*" is more than a single point of conversion; it is a moving, dynamic, ongoing way of life in responsiveness to God.

In the words of my friend Mike Breen, these three form the great relational triangle of "Up, In, and Out":

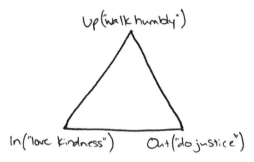

1. "*Do justice*" – our relationship "**Out**" to the world, characterized by a <u>missionary zeal</u>;

2. "*Love kindness*" – our relationships "**In**" toward others we know and love, demonstrated in <u>radical community</u>; and

3. "*Walk humbly*" – our relationship "**Up**" toward God, who desires from us <u>passionate spirituality</u>.

At any given point, a leader may look at his or her life and determine if s/he is living in a relationally balanced way. Often leaders get "out of whack" by demonstrating only two of the three. An example is an "Up/Out" leader who casts great vision and pushes hard and wide into the world, but who forgets to care for and build any sense of team ("In"). Great leaders remember all three.

The prophetic leader will always correct back to Micah's great triangle. So we can always ask: Am I living "Up" with God, "In" with key relationships, and "Out" toward the world?

NAHUM

GLOATING. DESPAIR. CONFIDENCE

"The Lord is slow to anger but great in power, and the Lord will by no means clear the guilty." – Nahum 1:3

Most of the book of Nahum's 47 verses are spent gloating over the fall of Israel's cruel and unscrupulous tormenters from Nineveh. When the Babylonian empire overtook Assyria toward the end of the seventh century B.C., Nineveh got a taste of her own medicine. And Nahum, like most of the nation, howled with delight at the humiliation of those who had tortured Israel.

For a century, Israel had wallowed in despair as an enslaved people. Now set free by a third party, they turned their rage full bore onto their hated former captors. For the most part, Nahum joins right in with the mockery. It is not pretty. Moreover, only a few decades after the recording of his taunting, the Babylonians turned on Israel, plunging them again into captivity.

But between the agony of despair and unseemliness of gloating, lies in Nahum a middle option that is more in line with the wider heart of biblical faith. He says, "*The Lord is slow to anger but great in power, and the Lord will by no means clear the guilty.*" These words are an affirmation of proper confidence in the providence of God to set all things right. There is no need to despair in temporary defeat, and no need to taunt in temporary victory when we have a confidence that God will set all things aright. So we have:

Despair   ←   **<u>Confidence</u>**   →   **Gloating**

At our best, leaders of biblical faith maintain a posture between a hopelessness that things will never work out, and arrogance that our victory is inevitable. We are neither gloomy in defeat nor triumphalist in victory. We neither view our captors/competitors as all-powerful, nor do we howl in delight at their defeat. Real battles can still be won or lost, and there are important things at stake in those battles. But after the D-Day of the cross of Jesus Christ, the outcome of the war is certain. Therefore, at all times and in all circumstances, we maintain a proper confidence in the merciful power of God to justify all accounts.

John P. Chandler   333

HABAKKUK 2

"Then the Lord answered me and said, "Write the vision and make it plain on tablets, so that a runner may read it. For there is still a vision for the appointed time; it speaks of the end, and does not lie. If it seems to tarry, wait for it; it will surely come, it will not delay. Look at the proud! Their spirit is not right in them, but the righteous will live by their faith."
– Habakkuk 2:2-4

Writing in a turbulent time, Habakkuk the prophet voices the fierce, questioning prayers of his people to God. They are the classic questions of theodicy: Why do the righteous suffer? Why is God silent when we pray? How long before things on earth are set right? The people are paralyzed by their questions, and God's response to Habakkuk for them is to *"write the vision and make it plain."* God's response is that the universe still makes sense and our behavior still matters. It is not for us to know the timing of God, but only for us to live in a humble and righteous way while we work alongside of God.

The genius of Habakkuk's leadership is that he takes perplexing and paralyzing questions from people and prayerfully responds to them with clarity. In basketball parlance, he tells people that they are not to guess the final score, but to play well on the next possession. "Do what's next," one coach says. The prophet coaches the people to do well what is next, what is right in front of them – and leave the final outcome of the world to God. Make it so plain that a passing runner can get the message without having to stop to decipher.

Great leaders don't attempt to be profound; they attempt to be clear. Complexity may dazzle but it does not mobilize. Clarity is not the same as being simplistic, but is a boiling down of what really matters that can only come on the far side of praying and working through complexity. The progression looks like this:

Difficult problems → Simplistic slogans →

Complexity → Prayerful intercession →

Clarity of leader → Mobilized people

We haven't led when we simply recognize the complexity of issues before us. We have led only once we come to the far side of that with a brevity and clarity that moves people to action in the next thing before them.

Exercise: *Where am I on this spectrum? Is it possible that I am overcomplicating a leadership situation before me? Ask God to give you clarity and brevity in how you think about responding, and clarity in how you communicate the challenge to those around you.*

ZEPHANIAH 1

BAD WINE

"At that time I will search Jerusalem with lamps, and I will punish the people who rest complacently on their dregs, those who say in their hearts, "The Lord will not do good, nor will he do harm." – Zephaniah 1:12

Praying the Prophets

Zephaniah is an unsparing prophet of judgment who proclaims a coming day of the Lord to a people grown idolatrous, syncretistic, and especially indifferent. He speaks most harshly to Israel's four leadership classes ("*officials, judges, prophets, priests,*" 3:3f) for their lack of the fear of God and his coming Day. John Calvin summarized Zephaniah's message by saying, "When the next house (the fall of neighboring nations) was on fire, how was it possible for you to sleep, except ye were extremely stupid?" But the leaders of Israel were asleep at the wheel, and the prophet said the whole nation was about to pay for their dereliction of duty.

The prophet's most interesting image of this failure of leadership is the description of unstirred wine. Bad leaders "*rest complacently on their dregs.*" They assume that God is uninvolved in the daily affairs of leaders and the nation, neither doing "*good*" nor "*harm.*" These leaders are thus unstirred by any need to align their decisions with the active involvement of God's guiding hand in the affairs of the nation. Zephaniah's word is against complacent, unspiritual, and indifferent leadership.

In the winemaking of the day, if the wine was not frequently stirred while fermenting, the bottom would become thick and sludge-like, while the top would take on the color of wine but not the flavor. Only a lazy, indolent, or careless winemaker would let this happen. A whole batch is ruined – the unfinished top without body, the congealed bottom moldy and unable to move. It is a picture of God's judgment on leaders whose lack of urgency, attentiveness, and diligence fails to stir a nation and leads to the ruin of both.

Leading can be like making wine. It takes a dependence on the God-given grape and weather, combined with a diligent and steady attention to cultivation and stirring by the winemaker.

John P. Chandler   339

HAGGAI 1

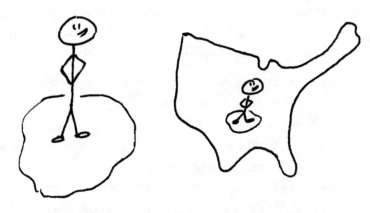

FROM LOCAL TO NATIONAL

"You have looked for much, and, lo, it came to little; and when you brought it home, I blew it away. Why? says the Lord of hosts. Because my house lies in ruins, while all of you hurry off to your own houses." **– Haggai 1:9**

Praying the Prophets

Haggai addresses the people of God who are trying to rebuild life after coming through the national crisis of Babylonian exile in the sixth century B.C. Commentator Richard Foster describes how devout God-followers were then to cultivate identity and express faith. *"After the people are home, but still under the domination of foreign powers, God ordains two institutions to stand at the heart of Jewish religious life: the synagogue ... and the restored temple."*

These are the two tick-tock impulses of a life of faith in the Old Testament – local, and national:

Local	National
synagogue	temple
rabbi/local pastor	priest/national spiritual leader
Law/Torah/Bible	liturgy/ritual
weekly worship	national festival/holiday
daily devotional	pilgrimage
family orientation	larger spiritual citizenship

A healthy faith rhythmically moves between these two. (Later, Jesus would radicalize this thinking by adding a third: the need to experience life with God not only locally and nationally, but in a radically personal way.)

Haggai writes prophetically because the people of God have withdrawn almost exclusively into the "local" sphere of expressing faith. It has become all about *"your houses"* and nothing about *"my house"* (the national temple). Any faith that becomes only local becomes narcissistic, xenophobic, and small.

As important as personal and communal ways of expressing our faith are, a leader can never allow people to let those be the only ways of living biblically. The people of the Book are also called to live out our life with God in trans-local ways. We are to be a light to the nations.

HAGGAI 2

COURAGE + WORK = SUPPLY

"...take courage, all you people of the land, says the Lord;
work, for I am with you, says the Lord of hosts ..."
– Haggai 2:4

In the Bible, God's people are summoned to "*take courage*" in times of anxiety, distress, emergency, great need. They can "*take courage*" based on God's readiness to help them. "*Take courage,*" Jesus says to his followers in John 16:33, "*I have conquered the world.*" Haggai says that God has been with the people since "*you came out of Egypt*" (v. 5). He reminds the people – economically uncertain, politically not in charge, shaky in their faith – that they can and must fearlessly "*take courage*" and get to "*work,*" because God's spirit "*abides among you.*"

If the people's part is to "*take courage* and *work,*" then God's part is to provide for the needs of the great rebuilding he desires. And the God above all gods promises to do so: "*I will shake all the nations, so that the treasure of all nations shall come, and I will fill this house with splendor, says the Lord of hosts*" (v. 7). God claims that all of the "*silver*" and "*gold*" (v. 8) of the earth belongs to heaven, and God will use it to "*give prosperity*" (v. 9) to those who courageously work.

God's <u>work</u> (rebuilding done by his people)
done in God's <u>way</u> (with trusting courage)
will never lack God's <u>supply</u> (the resources needed for the job)!

As philosopher Dallas Willard often says, "The guidance system takes over when the rocket leaves the launching pad, and the power steering works once the car is in motion." God has the "*silver and gold*" to complete his holy project of the healing and repair of all of creation. And God deploys those resources once his people have begun to "*take courage and work.*"

The leader always gets people to change their anxious attitudes (*take courage*), get to *work*, and trust that God will *give prosperity* when we do. Courage + work = supply.

John P. Chandler   345

ZECHARIAH 1

"Then the Lord showed me four blacksmiths. And I asked,
"What are they coming to do?" He answered, "These are the
horns that scattered Judah, so that no head could be raised;
but these have come to terrify them, to strike down the horns
of the nations that lifted up their horns against the land of
Judah to scatter its people." – Zechariah 1:20-21

Zechariah writes on the hinge of a new era in Judah, when the nation was emerging from a long and painful exile. The prophet envisions a new day, radically unlike previous decades spent under the thumb of oppressors. One of his gifts in the Bible is a series of eight imaginative, apocalyptic visions of God's work through his agents (human leaders) to stir up a new day of peace.

The second of these eight visions is of "*four horns*" (powerful enemies) and "*four blacksmiths*" (God's leaders). Simply and briefly, Zechariah is told that while the *horns* have bulled/bullied the city of God around for some time, God was raising up smiths to "*strike down*" these enemy forces who would "*scatter* and *terrify*" people who yearned to be free.

It is an arresting image of the work of leadership for our day. The work of the smith (and origin of its name) is to "smite." The primary competencies are the ability to conceptualize a desired product, physical strength to endure heat and pound on unyielding material, and relentlessness to work in a hard window of opportunity for change. The main competencies of a smith are forging and welding. Blacksmiths make malleable things which were formerly unchangeable. Their final products are not fine and delicate, but durable and strong. God, according to Zechariah, sends such blacksmith leaders against the agents that terrorize his people.

Certainly there is a "soft" side to leadership, where the leader is marked by traits of sensitivity. But make no mistake: in times of deep transition and in the face of powerful opposition, God always calls forth leaders who are blacksmiths. These leaders do the hard, hot, pounding work of banging on unyielding forces until a new and holy future is forged.

Exercise: *Is there something forceful, strong, and loud required of you and your leadership right now? Ask God to fortify you with the courage, strength, and perseverance to pound away at it.*

ZECHARIAH 3

"Then the angel of the Lord assured Joshua, saying, "Thus says the Lord of hosts: If you will walk in my ways and keep my requirements, then you shall rule my house and have charge of my courts, and I will give you the right of access among those who are standing here." – Zechariah 3:6-7

In Zechariah's eight visions of the new day that God will bring for the world, there are not only imaginative pictures about what the new city will look like, but also visions of who will rule and lead in it. Apparently God will change both the physical hardware and human software of this New Jerusalem.

Chapter 3 envisions Joshua, a leader whose grandfather and father were failed rulers, captives and victims of Babylonian oppressors. Joshua, who is dressed in *"filthy clothes"* (v. 3) and accused by Satan like a prosecuting attorney in the heavenly court (v. 1), looks as if he will fare no better in leading.

But in the vision, the angel of God intervenes and exchanges Joshua's dirty rags for *"festal apparel"* and a *"clean turban"* (vv. 4f). The symbolism is clear: by this work of divine grace, God will break the cycle of failed leadership and transform Joshua as a future ruler. God tells Joshua that if he will *"walk"* obediently and keep God's *"requirements,"* then he will gain the *"right of access"* to the court of heaven. The Lord will not only forgive Joshua's sins; he will also transform Joshua as a leader by granting him *"access"* to the ruler of the universe.

The most game-changing gift that God can give to a leader is communion with himself. By dealing with our legacy of dirt and failure, and in combination with our intentional path to honor and obey, God can make a jewel (v. 9) out of an ordinary leader like Joshua. When we have access to God, we have an open line of conversation with the Leader of all of history. This Leader is not only willing and able to deal with our own hearts, but also to guide and equip us to rule in a new city.

Thanks be to God, who through the person and work of Jesus Christ has given us open access to the throne of heaven, even as we work on earth!

John P. Chandler 349

ZECHARIAH 4

BEYOND
RESOURCES
AND
RESOLUTENESS

"Not by might, nor by power, but by my spirit, says the Lord of hosts." – Zechariah 4:6

Zechariah receives a vision of a lampstand and olive trees that fuel it. While the light from the lamp clearly symbolizes the witness of God's people, the lamp envisioned is unlike today's Jewish menorah or other lamps mentioned in the Bible. Commentator Elizabeth Achtemeier describes it this way:

> "Rather, as we know from similar lamps found by archaeologists, this is a cylindrical column, probably tapered upward, on top of which is an oil bowl .... On each side of the main bowl is an olive tree with a branch overshadowing the bowl, to which it feeds oil directly through a gold pipe. The whole lampstand is distinguished by the fact that it is made of costly metal and receives its liquid fuel directly from the olive trees without the necessity of human processing of the oil from the olives." (Achtemeier, p. 124)

Three times, the prophet asks the meaning of the vision. How do the people of God function as the lamp/light of God to the world?

God's oracle in response says, "Not by might and not by power." "Might" connotes force, means, wealth, efficiency, and other human resources. "Power" suggests human will, strength, purpose and other expressions of resoluteness. If the light of God is to shine to the world through human leaders, it will come from a source beyond human resources and human resoluteness. In short, the oil will be fed to the lamp through God's spirit. Here is direct, daily, and flowing correlation between tree and lamp, oil and light, God's fueling spirit and human leadership.

Light shines when and only when human leaders are organically connected to the Spirit of God, the divine Source beyond human resources and resoluteness. Armies can't forever rule the world and human will inevitably wavers. But when a leader is fed and led by the Spirit of God, the promise of Jesus is fulfilled: "I am the light of the world. Whoever follows me will never walk in darkness, but will have the light of life" (John 8:12). Leaders who would shine this light will be fueled by the Spirit.

ZECHARIAH 5

"I have sent it out, says the Lord of hosts, and shall enter the house of the thief, and the house of anyone who swears falsely by my name; and it shall abide in that house and consume it, both timber and stones." – **Zechariah 5:4**

Just before the final of Zechariah's eight visions – the coming of a messiah – the prophet is given two strange visions of cleansing in chapter 5. One (vv. 5-11) is a picture of a woman who personifies "*Wickedness*" being flown out of the land and deposited far away, quarantined in a place where people happily allow her to operate freely. The other (vv. 1-4) is a picture of a large banner (five by ten yards) with a curse on both sides. One side curses those "*everyone who steals*" and the other side "*everyone who swears falsely*" (v. 3). The work of the banner-curse is to enter every house where thievery and deception are the rule, to root out all social rot, and thus to cleanse the land of corruption in preparation for the rule of the Messiah.

In a conversation with young Argentine leaders, I asked which phrase of the Lord's Prayer was least helpful for their guidance. Their response across the board was, "*deliver us from evil*" (Matthew 6:13). One asked, "What happens if we don't pray that?" My instinctive response was, "Then you come to a gun fight armed only with a knife." Not a pleasant image, but neither is the necessary work of rooting out entrenched deception and corruption.

No leader can build on a social foundation riddled with corruption. No engineering or architecture matters if the footers are compromised by a culture of lying and stealing. And while every leader must be completely intolerant of corruption, let's face it: when it comes to dealing with evil, we need help from above. Ground troops need air superiority. We need the Spirit of God to confront and overcome the roaring lion of evil. It is not enough for a leader to pray for personal purity: "*lead us not into temptation.*" We need also to pray for divine power to root out the rot of entrenched corruption: "*deliver us from evil.*"

The good news is that when we pray "*deliver us from evil,*" the banner of God will go out ahead of us and work before us to cleanse the houses, purify the land, and carry wickedness far away. We need not crusade on our own. We can go in the power alongside of the One who, on the cross, showed final resolve and power to "*deliver us from evil.*"

John P. Chandler   353

ZECHARIAH 8

"Thus says the Lord of hosts: In those days ten men from nations of every language shall take hold of a Jew, grasping his garment and saying, "Let us go with you, for we have heard that God is with you." – Zechariah 8:23

There are four archetypal human motivators: survival, fear, hate, and love. Of these, only love has the power to compel us toward a long-term and harmonious society. For this reason, Zechariah's eight oracles climax in chapter 8 with four pictures of the Kingdom of God coming to reign on earth. This day when God's love rules will look like:

1. A public park (vv. 4f): where "*old men and old women*" sit in the streets with honor, and "*the streets of the city shall be full of boys and girls playing*";

2. A fruitful harvest (v. 12): where nature and society are in perfect harmony;

3. Transformed public ceremonies (v. 19): where public mourning rituals of "*fasting*" have now become "*cheerful festivals*" of celebration of the reign of "*love and peace*"; and

4. Everyone begs to be a part of it (vv. 20-23): other nations see the flourishing of this Kingdom and vigorously seek to be included.

No longer do the people of God need to go out as missionary witnesses to the world. Now, the world comes to them. The joyful life of this Kingdom looks so compelling, so magnetic, that every nation begs to be included as a part of it. Everyone grabs the garment of the people of God, saying, "*Let us go with you, for we have heard that God is with you.*" The final motivator for the rule of the Kingdom of God "*on earth as it is in heaven*" (Matthew 6:10) is a community so beautiful that all are drawn to be a part it. It works by attraction, not promotion.

And the highest form of leadership is likewise to motivate through compelling pictures of the preferred future of a community of love. Sure, anyone in charge can motivate by appealing to survival instinct, hate, or fear. We can promote and push and sell. But great leaders motivate by love. And the great visions of leaders are pictures of life so winsome that everyone begs to be a part of it.

ZECHARIAH 14

BELLS AND POTS

"On that day there shall be inscribed on the bells of the horses, "Holy to the Lord." And the cooking pots in the house of the Lord shall be as holy as the bowls in front of the altar." – Zechariah 14:20

Zechariah's final word to a discouraged people trying to rebuild their city after exile is a word of grace and hope. Yes, he has often spoken pointedly of judgment, for people need to know that justice exists, the world is ordered, human behavior matters, and all actions will be accounted for and reconciled in the end. But justice, while necessary, isn't sufficiently compelling. There must be, beyond justice, a vision of love, something grander than fairness.

The prophet's picture of this is a final day when God's rules rule, and any who want to be included in a community that lives that way are invited to do so. Any who wish to come and worship the Lord? Come, says the prophet, there is room for you!

In this ideal and final community, the *"bells on the horses"* and *"cooking pots"* are described as *"holy."* That is, even the implements of work in the fields and in kitchens are filled with the presence of God. Our work is now sacred, not meaningless, cursed toil. It is impossible to go anywhere – field, kitchen, street, or home – that is not a sacred place.

As the last book of the Bible puts it, *"I saw no temple in the city, for its temple is the Lord God Almighty and the Lamb"* (Revelation 21:22). Ultimately there will be no need for church because all of ordinary life will be filled with the presence of God. Our work, our homes – these places will be full of meaning and harmony, because they will be consecrated to God and filled with the close and holy presence of the Lord. Church everywhere! Communion everywhere!

Zechariah ends on this hopeful note of a community where home and field (work) are filled with meaning. And every leader who casts vision must help us see beyond justice and to see this place of hope. We long for a day when our ordinary lives are filled with meaning that comes from the close presence of God. Leaders, help us live into that day!

John P. Chandler   357

MALACHI 1

REPUTATION MANAGEMENT

"Cursed be the cheat who has a male in the flock and vows to give it, and yet sacrifices to the Lord what is blemished; for I am a great King, says the Lord of hosts, and my name is reverenced among the nations." – Malachi 1:14

The prophet Malachi writes in the context of a multicultural society, where quickie divorces were commonplace, and the identity of God's people was being eroded by regular, casual compromise. He lays the blame for this sorry situation squarely at the feet of spiritual leaders. These priests were whiny about their hardship (v. 2) and bored with their jobs (v. 13). They were cynical in outlook and mechanical in the exercise of their duties. Worst of all, these "spiritual leaders" seemed more concerned about their own reputations than the reputation of God. Making a great public show of their "*sacrifices*," they were actually giving leftover and blemished offerings, at little personal expense – and everyone knew it.

Why would a leader portray and pretend to give more than s/he actually gave? Why would a spiritual leader go through public rituals of sacrifice when clearly not having the heart for it? Why would someone put on a show of bringing a gift to God (see Acts 5, Ananias and Sapphira) which was of less value than advertised? Why would a spiritual leader risk corrupting public opinion of his or her faith through hypocritical behavior?

Malachi thunders against any spiritual leader who cares more about their own reputation than the reputation of the God we serve. He calls such behavior "*vain, corrupt, polluted, and despised.*" Those leaders thought of what they were doing as "reputation management." Malachi has another word (from the Lord) for it: "*Cursed be the cheat.*"

Leaders set the bar for sacrifice. When we pretend to sacrifice more than we actually do, it is easily detected, and fatally corrosive. To cheat on sacrificing erodes personal integrity and public opinion. To sacrifice well is worthy of our "*great King, the Lord of hosts.*"

John P. Chandler

MALACHI 2

GUARD. INSTRUCTOR. MESSENGER

"For the lips of a priest should guard knowledge, and people should seek instruction from his mouth, for he is the messenger of the Lord of hosts." – Malachi 2:7

Praying the Prophets

Malachi unsparingly blames the problems of his culture on the failure of its leaders, the priests. The prophet insists that every priest has an "Up/In/Out" set of leadership responsibilities:

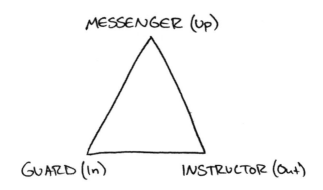

MESSENGER (Up)

GUARD (In)   INSTRUCTOR (Out)

Leaders are responsible to listen upward toward the Lord, and, as stewards of a vision greater than ourselves, to convey what we have heard as "_messengers._" We are also to "_guard_" a body of knowledge (Biblical teaching or Law) against cultural drift. And we are to give "_instruction_" to people so that all know what is expected of them and are held accountable to follow God-given direction.

This was not happening in Malachi's day. And the failure of priests/leaders then was demonstrated most obviously in the realm of marriage. People were adulterating God-given instructions about marriage. One result was a culture of "quickie divorces," the _"violence"_ of which is always manifested largely on women and children (vv. 14-16). Meanwhile, permissive, bored, lazy priests rubber stamped and failed to confront these widespread practices. They spent their time instead defending themselves and whining about theodicy (v. 17).

"Not many of you should become teachers, my brothers and sisters," says James 3:1, "for you know that we who teach will be judged with greater strictness." Malachi would agree. Leaders are responsible to live with personal uprightness, yes. But personal uprightness alone is insufficient. We are also required to serve "Up/In/Out" as messengers, guards, and instructors. We are stewards called to pass along God's instruction to those we lead. To fail to do so is to share in the blame of a compromised and violent culture.

Exercise: *What should be your "lead foot" for decisions you need to make today: as messenger, guard, or instructor?*

MALACHI 3

MEASURABLE GENEROSITY

"Will anyone rob God? Yet you are robbing me! But you say,
"How are we robbing you? In your tithes and offerings."
– Malachi 3:8

New York preacher Ernest Campbell fifty years ago observed that much objection to the Old Testament comes not from its gore – gruesome battles and so forth – but from the explicit nature of its commands. In the Old Testament, God tells people <u>exactly</u> what to do. And that makes some folk antsy, especially when you start talking about the discipline of tithing, or giving away one tenth of your money.

The three classic monastic vows of poverty, chastity, and obedience are responses to the belief that the critical realms of temptation for leaders pertain to money, sex, and power. Malachi charges spiritual leaders with unfaithfulness in each of these three matters. In chapter 3, the prophet specifically pinpoints the deception, stinginess, and lack of forthcoming honesty by leaders in financial matters. They are trying to gain credit for generosity by giving in a public manner. But they are not giving as generously as they should. (Ten per cent is a concrete, measurable standard.) They are failing to *bring the full tithe into the storehouse*" (v. 10). Malachi says their miserliness and deception (robbery!) will leave them exposed and unprepared when the day of the Lord comes and reckons all human accounts.

There was (and is today) much wiggling around the idea that God requires his people to give ten per cent of what they own/earn. The Bible brooks no waffling on it. The only way to grow a generous heart is to perform concrete, disciplined, specific, measurable acts of generosity. We overcome possessiveness by regularly giving away our possessions. We reduce money's grip on us by offering money back to God in tithes and releasing it in offerings. When we do so, God returns to us a far greater gift: "see *if I will not open the windows of heaven for you and pour down for you an overflowing blessing*" (v. 10). Indeed, heaven's windows swing on generosity's hinges.

John P. Chandler   365

To be a prophetic leader, it is not enough to be financially transparent and honest. We also have to be measurably generous. We cannot lead others to a *"land of delight"* where *"all nations will count you happy"* (v. 12) without personal, demonstrative giving. What a leader gives financially is not only fair game for public knowledge. It is also indispensable in refining the leader. No one can simultaneously rob and lead. We can never call people to sacrifice and generosity without ourselves having learned to live there first.

Exercise: *When I look at my paycheck and look at my offering check, am I giving at least ten per cent of what I earn directly back to the work of God? If so, how can I become generous beyond legalism in a concrete way today? If not, allow God to deal with your heart.*

MALACHI 4

"He will turn the hearts of parents to their children and the hearts of children to their parents, so that I will not come and strike the land with a curse." **– Malachi 4:6**

The last verse of the Old Testament is a fork in the road, a promise to the sheep and a threat to the goats (Matthew 25:31-45). To the *"arrogant and all evildoers"* (v. 1), indifferent practical atheists, Malachi promises a coming *"day of the Lord"* that will *"burn them up"* like *"stubble"* (vv. 1, 5). People of faith have been so squeamish about the last word of the Old Testament ending with the possibility that God will *"strike the land with a curse"* that countless versions of the Bible have rearranged the texts so that it doesn't end that way! But the prophet doesn't flinch. There will be a final reckoning. Our behavior matters. If you do what you want and believe there is no God to whom you will account ... well, I hope you know what you're doing. Sincere agnosticism won't count for much when the final fire comes.

However, in the same breath, Malachi has this promise to a faithful remnant who remembers God's *"statutes and ordinances"* (v. 4): God will send a prophet like Elijah (John the Baptist) before the *"great and terrible day of the Lord comes"* (v. 5). This will set off events that lead to the reconciliation of the *"hearts of parents"* and *"children."* Happiness and harmony within families ... all that is important transmitted from one generation to the next ... a final *shalom*! No wonder that on this day when the *"sun of righteousness shall rise with healing in its wings"* the faithful *"shall go out leaping like calves from the stall"* (v. 2). This *"sun of righteousness"* that burns the lazy will warm the devoted.

Until that final *"oven"* (v. 1), we wait. But leaders know that waiting for the goal is never a passive activity. There is work to do and we have choices to make while wait. We need help, but we are not helpless. Will the final fire burn us up, or warm us into a land of joy and reconciliation?

John P. Chandler

Acknowledgements

Time and space are the media through which God creates, and through which we create. I would like to thank the dear people who have given gifts of time and space for writing this book. The beloved community they offer to me is a sign of the in-breaking Kingdom of God!

It is a joy to be enfolded within the world Baptist family, and John Upton symbolizes to me everything I love about my tribe: a global and Kingdom perspective, highly relational, and likeable, effective leadership. He is not only President of the Baptist World Alliance and Executive Director for Virginia Baptists, but the best boss I have ever had or seen! Thanks to John and to all of my friends and colleagues in the Baptist General Association of Virginia for the blessing and encouragement to work on this project. A shout-out to all in the "Uptick" tribe who are "winning the first battle of the day" and "working from rest." Thanks to David Bailey for creative and concrete conversation. Special thanks to dear friends and strategic collaborators Jim Baucom and Laura McDaniel – your vision, laughter, and partnership mean the world to me.

Thanks for the gifts of friends in the Argentina Baptist Association, especially Daniel Carro, Andrés Forteza and Paula Rodriguez (and Enzo), Daniel Lafortiva and Lili Mazzoni, Gustavo Moccia, Esteban and Mariella Licatta, Raúl Scialabba, and Sonia Trivillin, a God-gifted teacher and translator.

Thanks also to Joshua DuBois, formerly of the White House's Office of Faith-based and Neighborhood Partnerships, for spurring the project and demonstrating collaborative leadership. Thanks to

Mike Breen, Steve Cockram, and all of the 3DM *oikos* for friendship, invitation/challenge, huddles, and for teaching the value of LifeShapes as a tool for discipleship. Thanks to my awesome community of faith, All Souls Charlottesville, especially to Jessica Luttrull for using God's gift of your art.

Finally, thanks to my sons, Preston and Roland, not only for Spanish inspiration, but for becoming great young spiritual leaders. (Mingo, you too!) And saving the best for last, thanks to the love of my life, Mary, for the idea to start this work, for the quiet time and space every morning to help me practice what I preach, and for the example of how to listen and respond to God with a generous heart.

"I thank my God every time I remember you, constantly praying with joy in every one of my prayers for all of you, because of your sharing in the gospel from the first day until now. I am confident of this, that the one who began a good work among you will bring it to completion by the day of Jesus Christ." – Philippians 1:3-6

Selected Bibliography

All Scripture quotes are from the New Revised Standard Version. Note: In some instances, I have included a quote or idea from someone by name without citing a specific source. When no source is cited, this indicates one of several possible situations: that

1. *the quote or idea was cited within a commentary of another author listed below on that particular biblical passage, or*
2. *I heard it from them first hand in a personal conversation or sermon, or*
3. *I heard it attributed to them second hand orally in a lecture or conversation.*

I have done this in an order to reduce footnoting distractions or when I am uncertain of the original source. I hope readers will appreciate this intent. Authors, speakers, and historical citations are noted in the index.

Achtemeier, Elizabeth. *Jeremiah,* Knox Preaching Guides, John Knox Press, Atlanta, GA, 1987.

___. *Nahum-Malachi,* Interpretation: A Bible Commentary for Teaching and Preaching, John Knox Press, Atlanta, GA, 1986.

Alfaro, Juan I. *Micah: Justice and Loyalty*, International Theological Commentary, Wm. B. Eerdmans Publishing Company, Grand Rapids, MI, 1989.

Anderson, Robert A. *Daniel: Signs and Wonders*, International Theological Commentary, Wm. B. Eerdmans Publishing Company, Grand Rapids, MI, 1984.

Ariely, Dan. *The Honest Truth About Dishonesty: How We Lie to Everyone—Especially Ourselves*, HarperCollins, New York, NY, 2012.

Bechtel, Carol M. *Esther*, Interpretation: A Bible Commentary for Teaching and Preaching, John Knox Press, Atlanta, GA, 2002.

Beeby, H. D. *Hosea: Grace Abounding*, International Theological Commentary, Wm. B. Eerdmans Publishing Company, Grand Rapids, MI, 1989.

Blenkinsopp, Joseph. *Ezekiel*, Interpretation: A Bible Commentary for Teaching and Preaching, John Knox Press, Atlanta, GA, 1990.

Breen, Mike. *Covenant and Kingdom: The DNA of the Bible*, 3DMinistries, Pawleys Island SC, 2011.
____ and Steve Cockram. *Building a Discipling Culture: How to Release a Missional Movement by Discipling People Like Jesus Did*, 3DM, Pawleys Island, SC, 2011.

Brueggemann, Walter. *Isaiah 1-39*, Westminster Bible Companion, Westminster John Knox Press, Louisville, KY, 1998.

John P. Chandler   373

___. *Isaiah 40-66,* Westminster Bible Companion, Westminster John Knox Press, Louisville, KY, 1998.

___. *Jeremiah 1-25: To Pluck Up, To Tear Down,* International Theological Commentary, Wm. B. Eerdmans Publishing Company, Grand Rapids, MI, 1988.

___. *Jeremiah 26-52: To Build Up, To Plant,* International Theological Commentary, Wm. B. Eerdmans Publishing Company, Grand Rapids, MI, 1991.

Cain, Susan. *Quiet: The Power of Introverts in a World That Can't Stop Talking,* Crown Publishers, New York, NY, 2012.

Claypool, John. *Tracks of a Fellow Struggler: Living and Growing Through Grief,* Morehouse Publishing, Harrisburg, PA, 2004.

Clements, R. E. *Jeremiah,* Interpretation: A Bible Commentary for Teaching and Preaching, John Knox Press, Atlanta, GA, 1988.

Coggins, Richard J., and S. Paul Re'emi. *Nahum, Obadiah, Esther: Israel among the Nations,* International Theological Commentary, Wm. B. Eerdmans Publishing Company, Grand Rapids, MI, 1985.

Collins, Jim, with Morten T. Hansen. *Great by Choice: Uncertainty, Chaos, and Luck – Why Some Thrive Despite Them All,* HarperCollins, New York, NY, 2011.

Covey, Steven. *The 7 Habits of Highly Effective People: Powerful Lessons in Personal Change,* Free Press; Revised edition, 2004.

Czeslaw, Milosz. *The Witness of Poetry*, Harvard University Press, Cambridge, MA, 1983.

DePree, Max. *Leadership Is An Art*. Doubleday, New York, NY, 1987.

Dobbs-Allsopp, F.W. *Lamentations*, Interpretation: A Bible Commentary for Teaching and Preaching, John Knox Press, Atlanta, GA, 2002.

Florida, Richard. *Who's Your City?: How the Creative Economy Is Making Where to Live the Most Important Decision of Your Life*, Basic Books, Philadelphia, PA, 2008.

Foster, Richard, and Dallas Willard, Walter Brueggemann. *The Life with God Bible*, HarperCollins, New York, NY, 1989.

Gammie, John G. *Daniel*, Knox Preaching Guides, John Knox Press, Atlanta, GA 1983.

Gowan, Donald E. *Ezekiel*, Knox Preaching Guides, John Knox Press, Atlanta, GA 1985.

Hauerwas, Stanley. *Naming the Silences: God, Medicine, and the Problem of Suffering*, Wm. B. Eerdmans Publishing Company, Grand Rapids, MI, 1990.

Kellerman, Barbara. *Bad Leadership: What It Is, Why It Happens, How it Matters*, Harvard Business School Publishing, Boston, MA, 2004.

Knight, George A. F. *Isaiah 40-55: Servant Theology*, International Theological Commentary, Wm. B. Eerdmans Publishing Company, Grand Rapids, MI, 1984.

____ and Friedemann W. Golka. *The Song of Songs & Jonah: Revelation of God*, International Theological Commentary, Wm. B. Eerdmans Publishing Company, Grand Rapids, MI, 1988.

____. *Isaiah 56-66: The New Israel*, International Theological Commentary, Wm. B. Eerdmans Publishing Company, Grand Rapids, MI, 1983.

Martin-Achard, Robert and S. Paul Re'emi. *Amos & Lamentations: God's People in Crisis,* International Theological Commentary, Wm. B. Eerdmans Publishing Company, Grand Rapids, MI, 1984.

Milosz, Czeslaw. *The Witness of Poetry,* Harvard University Press, Cambridge, MA, 1984.

Niebuhr, H. Richard. *Christ and Culture,* Harper and Row, New York, NY, 1951.

Ogden, Graham S., and Richard R. Deutsch. *Joel & Malachi: A Promise of Hope – A Call to Obedience,* International Theological Commentary, Wm. B. Eerdmans Publishing Company, Grand Rapids, MI, 1987.

Peterson, Eugene. *Five Smooth Stones for Pastoral Work*, Eerdmans, Grand Rapids, MI, 1980.

Rath, Tom. *Vital Friends: The People You Can't Afford to Live Without*, Gallup Press, Princeton, NJ, 2006.

Roam, Dan. *The Back of the Napkin (Expanded Edition): Solving Problems and Selling Ideas with Pictures,* Penguin Group, New York, NY, 2009.

Roth, Wolfgang. *Isaiah,* Knox Preaching Guides, John Knox Press, Atlanta, GA 1988.

Stuhlmueller, Carroll. *Haggai & Zechariah: Rebuilding with Hope,* International Theological Commentary, Wm. B. Eerdmans Publishing Company, Grand Rapids, MI, 1988.

Szeles, Maria Eszenyei. *Habakkuk & Zephaniah: Wrath and Mercy,* International Theological Commentary, Wm. B. Eerdmans Publishing Company, Grand Rapids, MI, 1987.

Tillich, Paul. *Systematic Theology: Three Volumes in One,* University Of Chicago Press 1st edition, Chicago, IL, 1967.

Towner, W. Sibley. *Daniel,* Interpretation: A Bible Commentary for Teaching and Preaching, John Knox Press, Atlanta, GA, 1984.

Tufte, Edward R. *Beautiful Evidence,* Graphics Press, first edition July 2006.

____. *Envisioning Information,* Graphics Press, 1990.

____. *Visual Explanations: Images and Quantities, Evidence and Narrative,* Graphics Press, 1997.

Vawter, Bruce and Leslie J. Hoppe. *Ezekiel: A New Heart,* International Theological Commentary, Wm. B. Eerdmans Publishing Company, Grand Rapids, MI, 1991.

Ward, James M. *Amos/Hosea,* Knox Preaching Guides, John Knox Press, Atlanta, GA 1981.

Westermann, Claus. *Isaiah 40-66:A Commentary,* Old Testament Library, translated by Herbert Hartwell,The Westminster Press, Philadelphia, PA, 1969.

Widyapranawa, S. H. *Isaiah 1-39:The Lord is Savior,* International Theological Commentary,Wm. B. Eerdmans Publishing Company, Grand Rapids, MI, 1990.

Willard, Dallas. *Hearing God Through the Year (Through the Year Devotionals), Updated and Expanded: Developing a Conversational Relationship with God,* IVP Books, 2004, 2012.

___. *The Spirit of the Disciplines: Understanding How God Changes Lives,* HarperOne, 1990.

___. *In Search of Guidance: Developing a Conversational Relationship with God,* HarperCollins, 1993.

Table of Scripture Chapters

Isaiah 1, 2, 3-4, 5, 6, 8, 9, 10, 11, 12, 13, 14, 16, 22, 23, 24, 26, 28, 30, 32, 33, 35, 36, 37, 38-39, 40, 41, 42, 43, 44, 45, 46, 47, 49, 50, 51, 53, 55, 56, 57, 58, 61, 64, 65, 66 (45)

Jeremiah 1, 2, 6, 9, 12, 13, 14-15, 15-16, 18, 20, 22, 23, 24, 25, 26, 27-28, 29, 30, 31, 32, 33, 34-35, 36, 37-39, 39-40, 42-43, 44-45, 46, 49, 50-51, 52 (31)

Lamentations 1, 2, 3 (3)

Ezekiel 3, 4-5, 6-7, 8-11, 12, 13-14, 15, 16, 17, 18, 20, 22, 24, 25, 26-28, 29-32, 33, 34, 36, 37, 40-42, 43, 44, 46, 47-48 (25)

Daniel 1, 2, 3, 4, 5, 6, 7, 8, 9, 11, 12 (11)

Hosea 1-3, 4, 5, 6, 7, 8, 9-10, 1, 12, 13, 14 (11)

Joel 2 (1)

Amos 2, 3, 4, 5, 6, 7, 8, 9 (8)

Obadiah (1)

Jonah 1, 3 (2)

Micah 2, 3, 4, 6 (4)

Nahum (1)

Habakkuk 2 (1)

Zephaniah (1)

Haggai 1, 2 (2)

Zechariah 1, 3, 4, 5, 8, 14 (6)

Malachi 1, 2, 3, 4 (4)

Praying the Prophets

Index